Easy Lotus® Notes 4.5

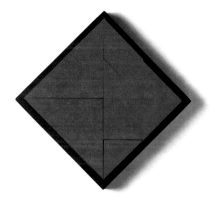

Elaine Marmel

Easy Lotus Notes 4.5

Library of Congress Catalog Card Number: 96-70768

International Standard Book Number: 0-7897-0946-5

99 98   8 7 6 5 4

Interpretation of the printing code: the rightmost number of the first series of numbers is the year of the book's printing; the rightmost number of the second series of numbers is the number of the book's printing. For example, a printing code of 97-1 shows that the first printing of the book occurred in 1997.

Screen reproductions in this book were created by means of the program Collage Complete from Inner Media, Inc., Hollis, NH.

This book was produced digitally by Macmillan Computer Publishing and manufactured using computer-to-plate technology (a film-less process) by GAC/Shepard Poorman, Indianapolis, Indiana.

Credits

President
Roland Elgey

Editorial Services Director
Elizabeth Keaffaber

Publishing Director
Lynn E. Zingraf

Managing Editor
Michael Cunningham

Acquisitions Editor
Martha O'Sullivan

Product Development Specialist
Melanie Palaisa

Technical Editors
Steve Kern
Jane Calabria

Production Editor
Mark Enochs

Director of Marketing
Lynn E. Zingraf

Cover Designers
Dan Armstrong
Barbara Kordesh

Designers
Barbara Kordesh
Ruth Harvey

Technical Specialist
Nadeem Muhammed

Indexers
Christopher Barrick
Craig Small

Production Team
Erin M. Danielson
Jessica Ford
Trey Frank
Amy Gornik
Christy Hendershot
Kaylene Riemen
Julie Searls
Paul Wilson

Composed in *Syntax* and *New Century Schoolbook* by Que Corporation

About the Author

Elaine Marmel is President of Marmel Enterprises, Inc., an organization that specializes in technical writing and software training. Elaine spends most of her time writing and is the author of several books on Word for Windows, Word for the Mac, Quicken for Windows, Quicken for DOS, 1-2-3 for Windows, and Excel. Elaine also is a contributing editor to *Inside Timeslips* and *Inside Peachtree for Windows*, monthly magazines published about Timeslips, a time and billing package, and Peachtree for Windows, an accounting package.

Elaine left her native Chicago for the warmer climes of Florida (by way of Cincinnati, OH; Jerusalem, Israel; Ithaca, NY; and Washington, D.C.) where she basks in the sun with her PC and her cats, Cato and Watson. Elaine also sings in the Toast of Tampa, an International Champion Sweet Adeline barbershop chorus.

Trademark Acknowledgments

Contents

Contents

Part V: Notes and Discussion Groups 162

Part VI: Notes and Traveling 182

Part VII: Setting Notes Preferences 204

Part VIII: Reference 220

Index 224

Introduction

What You Can Do with Lotus Notes

You can use Notes to communicate with others via electronic mail (e-mail). The scheduling features in Notes help you manage your time. Notes also provides a document management system. And, you can use Notes to track document-based discussions between individuals. Specifically, Lotus Notes has the following benefits:

- **Multi-platform.** Lotus Notes can run on Macintoshes, Windows, UNIX, and OS/2 machines at the same time and access the same information.

- **Notes Mail.** Notes is also a complete electronic mail package. You can easily send messages to and receive messages from any other Notes user on your network. You can attach documents to Notes mail messages and also send files and multimedia messages with audio and video characteristics.

- **Notes Time Management.** Notes contains a Calendar you can use to schedule appointments, multi-day events, meetings, reminders, and anniversaries. Using the To Do list in Notes, you can prioritize and keep track of things you need to do and, if you want, show the To Do list items on your calendar.

- **Databases.** You can make use of databases that Notes automatically creates for you, such as the Mail database, which holds all your mail messages. And, because Notes databases are "free-form" containers of information, you might use a Notes database (a group discussion database) that contains documents that discuss a particular topic. Finally, your company may use Notes to store information such as paper-based forms that are used company-wide.

- **Database replication.** Replication allows you to copy one database across multiple Notes servers. For example, if your company has a database that lists all of its employees, your administrator might want that database replicated to all servers in your Notes network so the servers all have the same version of the database.

You also can replicate all or part of a database from the server to your own computer. That way, you can work in the database when you're not connected to the Notes server, which is very useful for those who work away from the office. Later, you can replicate your local database back to the server to update the database on the server.

- **Security.** Lotus Notes has a strong, highly integrated security system that limits the access privileges for databases on your Notes networks.

- **Internet Access.** If you are using Notes Release 4.0 or higher, you can access the Internet. Connecting to and using the Internet is a large topic—and beyond the scope of this book. If you want to use the Internet, see your Notes Administrator for instructions.

Basic Notes Concepts

Before you read this book, you should be familiar with a few basic terms.

Notes uses the term *database* to refer to compartmentalized information in a single area of interest that you might want to share. This concept is really important, because Notes databases are not like traditional databases. For purposes of understanding Notes databases, think of databases as containers that hold similar information.

A *view* is the fundamental way to see information in a Notes database. Views summarize Notes documents in an easy-to-read format. You can customize views and use them to see different pieces of information in documents. Views are particularly useful for managing documents, since you can see a list of all available documents to update, add, or delete.

Notes databases store information in *documents*. You create Notes documents that are based on forms. A form is a customizable screen that is the basis of every document. Each form contains specific fields, and a field is the basic unit to store information in Notes. You'll find various types of fields on forms for text, dates, numbers, and graphics. The appearance of a Notes document depends on the form. Some forms have body and date fields, and others require specific words or user names. Each database has its own forms that are based on how the database will be used.

Task Sections

The Task sections include numbered steps that tell you how to accomplish certain tasks such as sending a mail message or creating a document. The numbered steps walk you through a specific example so you can learn the task by doing it.

Big Screen

At the beginning of each task is a large screen that shows how the computer screen will look after you complete the procedure that follows in that task. Sometimes, the screen shows a feature discussed in that task, such as a shortcut menu.

TASK 3

Navigating in Notes

"Why would I do this?"

Each task includes a brief explanation of why you would benefit from knowing how to accomplish the task.

"Why would I do this?"

While you can use either the keyboard or the mouse to navigate Notes, navigation is faster and easier with the mouse. To use the mouse, point at the database, menu, or command, and click. The number of times you click depends on what you're doing; to choose menus and commands, click once. To open a database, double-click. To display a quick menu, right-click.

To use the keyboard, you'll use the underscored letters (called *hot keys*) you see in menu and command names.

In this task, you'll learn to open menus, choose commands, and open and close your personal address book, which is a Notes database. Both keyboard and mouse methods are in this task, but in future tasks, you'll use the "easiest" method available.

8

Step-by-Step Screens

Each task includes a screen shot for each step of a procedure. The screen shot shows how the computer screen will look at each step in the process.

Task 3: Navigating in Notes

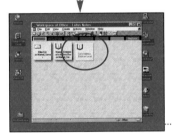

1 Select your personal address book database. Using the mouse, click the icon in the Workspace. The title of the address book appears in blue. Your personal address book contains your name and the words **on Local**. In the figure, Criz's Address Book on Local is the personal address book.

Missing Links

Many tasks contain Missing Link notes that tell you a little more about certain procedures. These notes define terms, explain other options, refer you to other sections when applicable, and so on.

2 Open your personal address book database. With the mouse, double-click the icon for your personal address book database. Using the keyboard, press **Enter** to open the selected database.

Missing Link

Later, you'll learn about other databases. Good news: you open every database the same way.

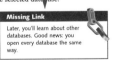

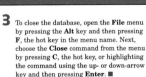

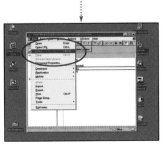

3 To close the database, open the **File** menu by pressing the **Alt** key and then pressing **F**, the hot key in the menu name. Next, choose the **Close** command from the menu by pressing **C**, the hot key, or highlighting the command using the up- or down-arrow key and then pressing **Enter**. ■

Puzzled?

If you open the wrong menu, press **Esc** to close the menu and press a different hot key. Or, to quickly close any window in Notes, press **Esc**.

Puzzled? Notes

You may find that you performed a task that you didn't want to do after all. The Puzzled notes tell you how to undo certain procedures or get out of a situation you didn't mean to get into.

9

PART I

Lotus Notes Basics

1 Starting Lotus Notes

2 Understanding Workspace Pages

3 Navigating in Notes

4 Using the Action Bar and the SmartIcon Bar

5 Using Context-Sensitive Notes Help

6 Understanding the Help Index and Searching Help

7 Changing the Size of the Notes Window

8 Exiting Lotus Notes

PART I OF THIS BOOK INTRODUCES you to Lotus Notes. You learn how to start and exit Notes, how to navigate within Notes, and how to use Notes Help functions. You also learn how to change the size of the Notes window.

To start Lotus Notes, you should have the program installed on your hard disk. We have included a set of installation steps at the back of the book for installing Notes on a workstation running the Windows 95 operating system. If you need additional help installing Lotus Notes on your hard drive, see your systems administrator or the documentation for the program. Once Notes is installed, the icon to run it appears, by default, in the Lotus Applications folder when you highlight Programs on the Start menu. While Notes is running, you can take advantage of Windows features, such as using the Clipboard and accessing a central printer.

When you first start Notes, you'll see the Notes Workspace. The Notes Workspace consists of a series of tabs called Workspace pages. You use these Workspace pages to organize the databases you use in Notes.

You move around in Notes using either the keyboard or the mouse. Although you can perform most of the tasks with keyboard commands, you will probably prefer the mouse, because the mouse makes it easy to access the various parts of Notes. With the mouse, you can select different ways to view the information in your databases (called database views), access and read documents, and maneuver through the various Notes screens. SmartIcons and the Action bar appear toward the top of the Notes screen. The Action bar and the SmartIcon bar contain shortcuts that save you time when you perform commands such as opening a document, sending mail, and underlining text. You click a button on either bar with the mouse to perform the command.

Notes also contains Help. If you would like more information about any screen or prompt within Notes, help is only a single keystroke away— just press F1. The Help information answers general questions about the current screen or prompt.

In addition to the single-key Help, Notes includes an indexed Help database. You can search this database for any Notes-related topic or command. The Notes Help index offers thorough descriptions of almost all the features and commands in Notes. Using your mouse, you can scroll through a directory of all available topics to find the desired Notes Help entry.

You also can search the Help database for entries using full or partial text strings. The Notes Help index is a great reference tool for learning how to access many of the intermediate and advanced features of Lotus Notes.

As in most other Windows programs, you can move, minimize, maximize, and resize the Notes window as you like.

The tasks that follow teach you the basic skills you need to use Lotus Notes effectively.

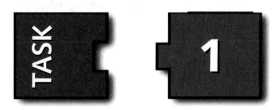

TASK 1

Starting Lotus Notes

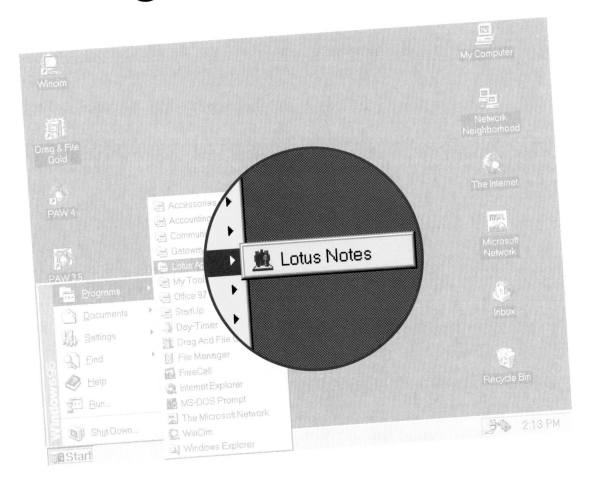

"Why would I do this?"

In Windows 95, you start Lotus Notes from the Programs menu on the Start menu. Typically, the installation process places Notes in the Lotus Applications Folder.

In this task, you'll learn how to start Notes, so turn on your computer.

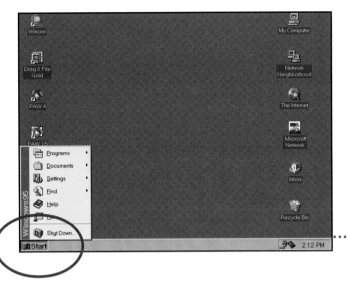

1 Click the **Start** button to display the Start menu.

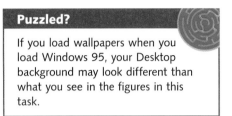

Puzzled?

If you load wallpapers when you load Windows 95, your Desktop background may look different than what you see in the figures in this task.

2 Slide the mouse onto the **Programs** menu. Windows displays the Programs menu choices, which will be different on each computer. The choices on the Programs menu depend on the programs loaded on your computer.

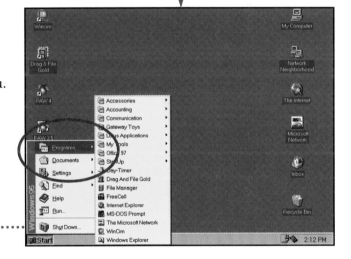

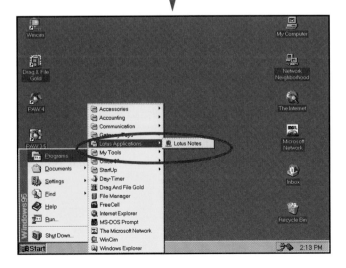

3 Highlight the folder containing Lotus Notes. Typically, you'll find Notes in the Lotus Applications folder. Click **Lotus Notes** once with the left mouse button. Notes starts, and the Notes Workspace appears on-screen. You learn more about the Workspace in the next task. ■

TASK 2

Understanding Workspace Pages

"Why would I do this?"

Each time you start Notes, you must enter a password, and you see the Notes Workspace in the background. The Workspace includes the menus, the SmartIcon bar just below the menus, the tabbed pages which contain icons that represent databases you can open in Notes, and the status bar at the bottom of the screen. You use tabbed Workspace pages to organize the databases you use in Notes, perhaps by subject, with one tab for mail, one for discussion groups, and so on.

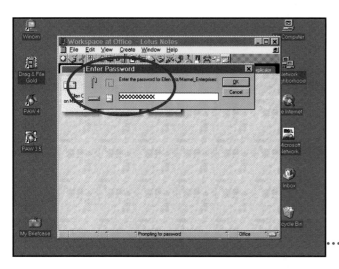

1 Notes will prompt you for your password once the Workspace appears on-screen. Enter the password your administrator gave you and click **OK**.

> **Puzzled?**
>
> As you enter your password, Notes fills the text box with X's to hide what you type.

2 The first Workspace page contains mail-related database icons: your mail database, the server address book, and your personal address book.

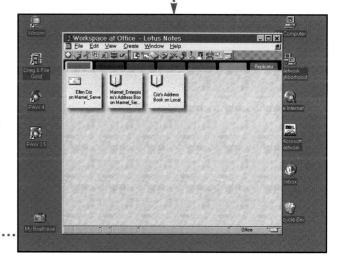

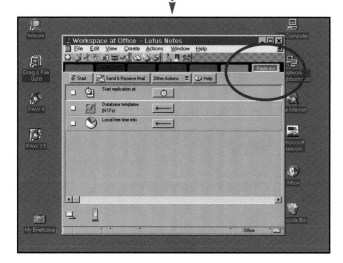

3 Click the tab of a Workspace page to display the contents of that page. Initially, all tabs are blank except the first and last ones, and all tabs are untitled except the last one. ■

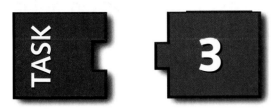

TASK

3

Navigating in Notes

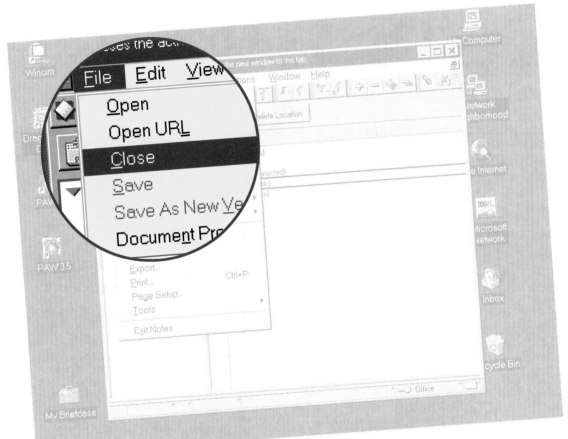

"Why would I do this?"

While you can use either the keyboard or the mouse to navigate Notes, navigation is faster and easier with the mouse. To use the mouse, point at the database, menu, or command, and click. The number of times you click depends on what you're doing; to choose menus and commands, click once. To open a database, double-click. To display a quick menu, right-click.

To use the keyboard, you'll use the underscored letters (called *hot keys*) you see in menu and command names.

In this task, you'll learn to open menus, choose commands, and open and close your personal address book, which is a Notes database. Both keyboard and mouse methods are in this task, but in future tasks, you'll use the "easiest" method available.

12

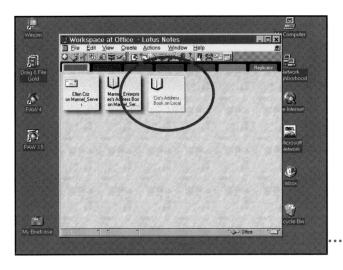

1 Select your personal address book database. Using the mouse, click the icon in the Workspace. The title of the address book appears in blue. Your personal address book contains your name and the words **on Local**. In the figure, Criz's Address Book on Local is the personal address book.

2 Open your personal address book database. With the mouse, double-click the icon for your personal address book database. Using the keyboard, press **Enter** to open the selected database.

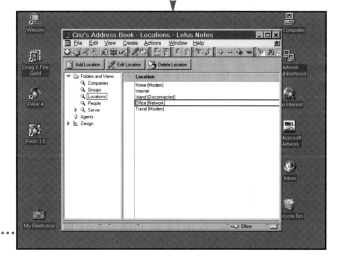

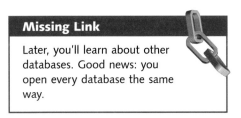

Missing Link

Later, you'll learn about other databases. Good news: you open every database the same way.

3 To close the database, open the **File** menu by pressing the **Alt** key and then pressing **F**, the hot key in the menu name. Next, choose the **Close** command from the menu by pressing **C**, the hot key, or highlighting the command using the up- or down-arrow key and then pressing **Enter**. ■

Puzzled?

If you open the wrong menu, press **Esc** to close the menu and press a different hot key. Or, to quickly close any window in Notes, press **Esc**.

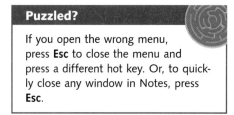

 **4**

Using the Action Bar and the SmartIcon Bar

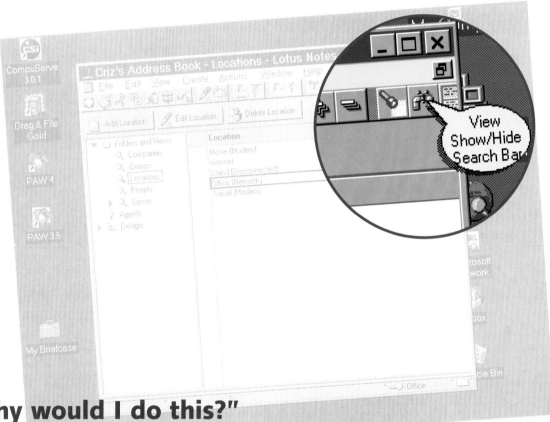

"Why would I do this?"

Buttons on the Action bar and the SmartIcon bar provide alternative, shorter ways to choose a command in Notes. You must use the mouse to choose an Action bar button or a SmartIcon. By default, SmartIcons appear under the Notes menu bar and the Action bar appears immediately below the SmartIcon bar when you are viewing a database; you won't see the Action bar while viewing the Workspace.

When you use a SmartIcon or an Action bar button, you don't have to pull down a menu and choose a command; you simply click the button or SmartIcon. The actions performed by Action bar buttons are written on the button. To determine the purpose of any particular SmartIcon, use the mouse to point at it; Notes will display a bubble describing the SmartIcon's purpose. By the way, the bubble is called "balloon help."

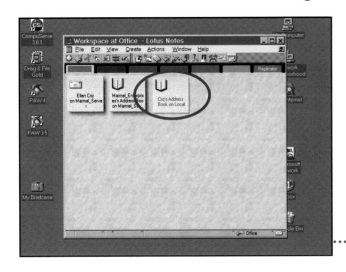

1 Open your Personal Address Book database.

2 Find the View Show/Hide Search Bar SmartIcon.

Puzzled?

Remember, when you point at any SmartIcon with the mouse, Notes will display a bubble that describes the SmartIcon's function.

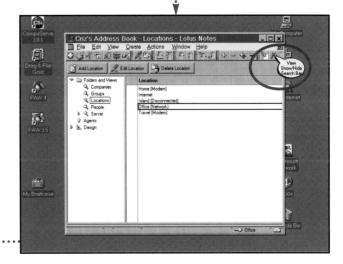

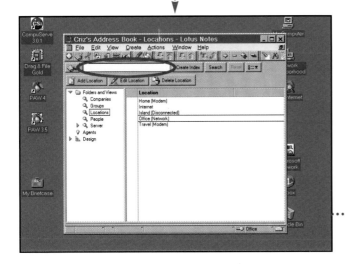

3 Click the View Show/Hide Search Bar SmartIcon to display the Search Bar.

Missing Link

You use the Search Bar to find information in a database; you'll learn more about the Search Bar in Part IV, Using Notes Databases and Documents.

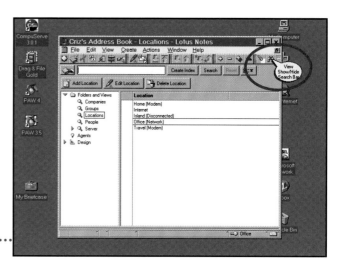

4 Close the Search Bar by clicking the View Show/Hide Search Bar SmartIcon again.

5 To display the Search Bar using the menus, open the **View** menu and choose the **Search Bar** command.

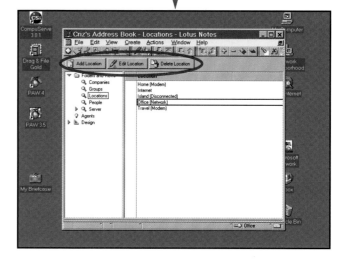

6 Action bar buttons appear below Smart-Icons in a database; their purpose is easy to identify because the action appears on the button. ■

Using Context-Sensitive Notes Help

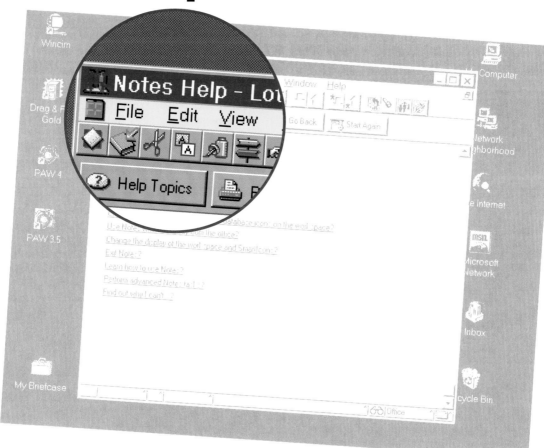

"Why would I do this?"

Notes Help is available anywhere within Notes. If you have a question about any prompt, screen, or message, press the **F1** key. Pressing F1 displays context-sensitive help; you'll see a Notes Help screen on the item currently select-ed. You may see, in some boxes, a button containing a question mark in the upper right corner of a box or a button containing the word Help. Clicking that button is the same as press-ing F1.

Task 5: Using Context-Sensitive Notes Help

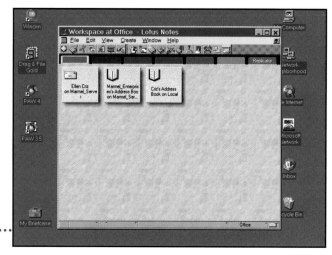

1 Click anywhere on the gray Notes Workspace to select it.

2 Press the **F1** key to request help on the item you have selected: the Notes workspace. Notes Help displays the Help window and a list of help topics, underlined in green, pertaining to the item you selected.

Puzzled?

By default, Help is stored on the server. Because the Help database is stored on the server, you may need to type your password to access it. After you access the server for the first time during a Notes session, you won't need to enter your password again.

3 To display the help associated with any topic, click that topic. As you point at the topic, the mouse pointer will change to a hand. ■

Missing Link

To close the help screen, press Ctrl+W, or open the **File** menu and choose the **Close** command. You'll see the Notes Help database added to the workspace tab.

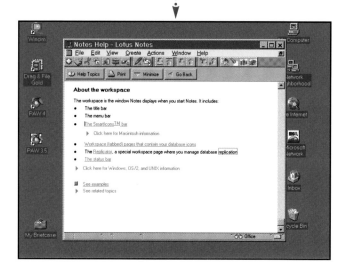

TASK 6

Understanding the Help Index and Searching Help

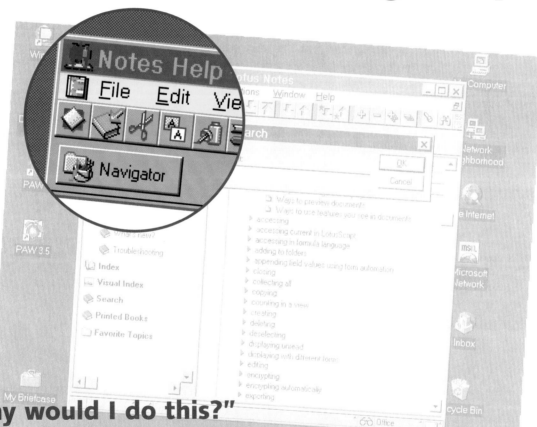

"Why would I do this?"

Another helpful feature of Notes Help is the index, which lists Help topics by subject. You can use the Notes Help index the same way you would use the index of a book to find information on such topics as opening a database, sending Notes Mail, or changing your Notes password. You can search the Help database in two ways: by scrolling and by using the Quick Search feature—you'll probably find the second method faster, as its name indicates.

The Help window you see looks different than the one that appears when you press F1; down the left side (called the Navigator pane), you see books with titles next to them. The open book is the Index. The topics associated with the open book appear on the right side of the window (called the View pane). And, the techniques you'll learn here about using the Help Index apply to any of the books you see on the left side of the window.

1 Double-click the **Notes Help** database icon or open the **Help** menu and choose **Help Topics**.

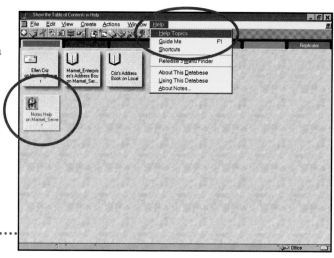

Puzzled?

For this figure, I moved my Help database so that you could see everything. You can move database icons on the Workspace tab by dragging them.

2 Notes displays the Help window.

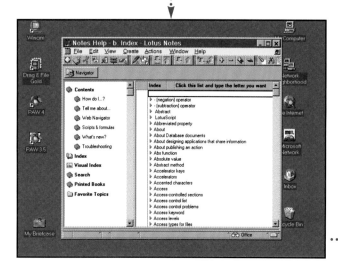

3 Use the scroll bar at the right edge of the screen to move the topics in the window until you see a topic that interests you and click that topic. In the figure, I chose Documents as the topic. Click the arrow next to the topic.

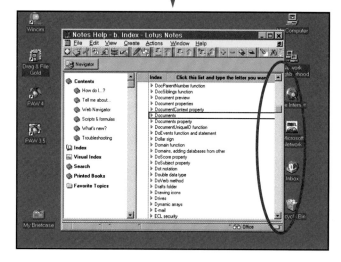

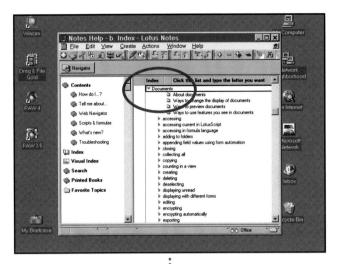

4 You see the list of available Help topics and Help documents, and the arrow next to the topic is now pointing down. To display a help document, double-click the small document icon next to the topic in the right side of the window.

> **Missing Link**
>
> You'll see an icon that looks like a piece of paper next to Help documents; you'll see another arrow next to additional Help topics.

5 Notes displays the Help document you selected in the window. To see the list of topics related to the document you opened, click **See related topics** at the bottom of the document window.

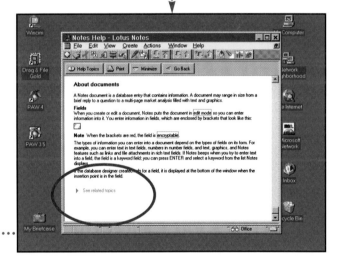

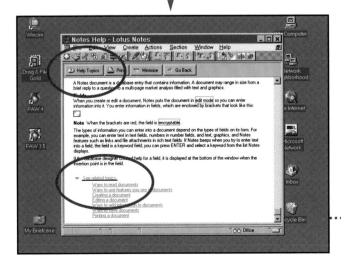

6 A list of related topics is displayed. You can jump to a related topic by clicking it. Click the **Help Topics** button on the Action bar to return to the Help index.

.

Task 6: Understanding the Help Index and Searching Help

7 To search the Help database instead of scrolling through it, type the first few letters of the topic for which you want to search. In the example, I typed **sen** to search for information on sending mail. When you type, Notes displays the Quick Search dialog box containing the letters you typed. When the Quick Search dialog box contains the letters for which you want to search, choose **OK**.

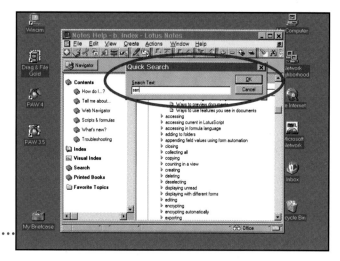

Missing Link

If you want to narrow the search further, type additional characters.

8 In the window on the right, Notes displays the title of the first subject that matches the letters you typed in the Quick Search dialog box. ■

Puzzled?

When you finish using the Help database, open the **File** menu and choose the **Close** command.

Changing the Size of the Notes Window

"Why would I do this?"

You can resize Notes to fit your screen. You can maximize the Notes window, or you can minimize the Notes window so that Notes appears as an icon on the taskbar. To resize the Notes window, use buttons located in the upper right corner of the window. The Minimize button looks like a flat line at the bottom of the button; the Maximize button contains an icon that looks like a window.

Task 7: Changing the Size of the Notes Window

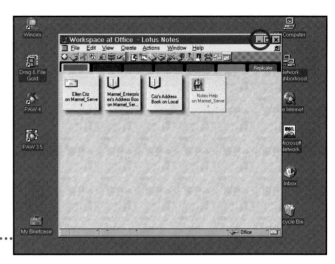

1 Click the **Minimize** button once.

2 Notes appears only as a button titled Workspace at Office on the Windows taskbar at the bottom of the screen.

> **Puzzled?**
>
> The actual words you see in the taskbar depend on "where" you were in Notes before you minimized. If you had opened a database in Notes before you minimized, you would see the title of that database in the taskbar.

3 To redisplay the Notes window again, click the Notes button in the taskbar at the bottom of the screen. Or, right-click the Notes button on the taskbar and choose the **Restore** command. The Notes window appears on-screen again.

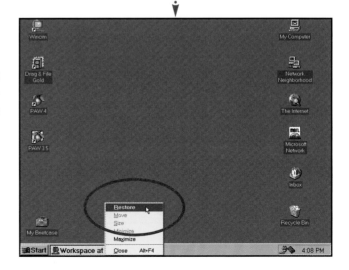

24

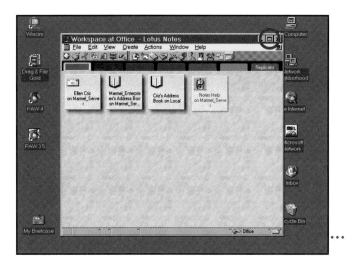

4 To enlarge Notes so that it fills the entire screen, click the **Maximize** button. The icon on the Maximize button is intended to look like a window with a title bar.

5 When you click the **Maximize** icon, Notes fills the screen, and Windows replaces the Maximize button with the Restore button. ■

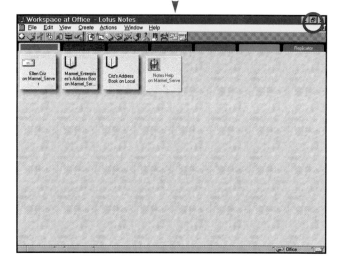

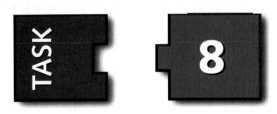

Exiting Lotus Notes

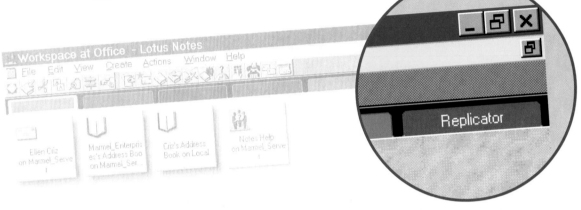

"Why would I do this?"

When you finish working in Notes, or when you intend to shut down your computer, you should close Notes. Closing Notes ensures that your data is saved correctly and that the program does some necessary housekeeping tasks.

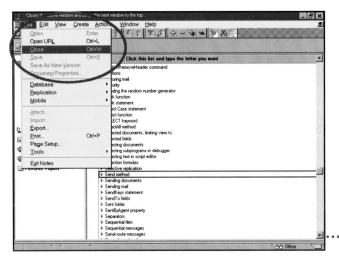

1 If you have any databases open, close them by opening the **File** menu and choosing the **Close** command.

Puzzled?

If you have open or unsaved documents, Notes will remind you to save the documents before you exit the program.

2 To close the program, click the **X** in the upper right corner of the screen. Notes shuts down and Windows redisplays the Desktop. ■

Missing Link

You can also close Notes by clicking **File** in the menu bar and then clicking **Exit Notes**.

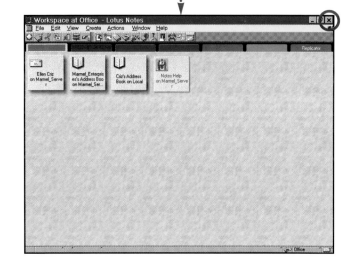

PART II

Using Notes Mail

NOW THAT YOU ARE FAMILIAR with the basics of Lotus Notes, you can start taking advantage of specific Notes features. One of the most important features is e-mail, referred to as Notes Mail.

In Part II, you learn about Notes Mail. You learn how to open your personal Mail database, view and read your messages, and organize your messages. You also learn how to use Notes Mail to print mail messages, share documents, respond to messages, forward mail to other Notes users, create a new mail message, and send carbon copies of a message. Finally, you'll learn about the Public and Personal Address books.

Your Notes Mail is a unique database in your Workspace; only you can access it unless you give others the privilege of accessing it, as you'll learn in Part VI. The Mail database does, however, have some characteristics in common with all Notes databases. For example, most of the time, the screen divides into two panes. The pane on the left, the Navigation pane, shows available views. Notes doesn't use the traditional folder icon for all of these views; for example, the Inbox appears as a tray. The pane on the right, the View pane, shows the contents of a particular view. As you click an icon in the Navigation pane, the menus at the top of the screen, the Action bar buttons, and the view pane will change. And, sometimes, you'll also see a Preview pane at the bottom of the screen. The Preview pane lets you look at a document you highlight in the View pane—without opening the document. You'll learn more about views in Part IV.

When you start getting a lot of mail, you'll need to know how to organize your mail messages. You can place mail in folders (either folders already available or folders you create) for future reference or delete unnecessary letters. You also can sort incoming and outgoing mail by size, date, sender, and category, making it easier for you to locate a particular mail message later.

Any time you delete a message, Lotus Notes initially marks the message for deletion instead of immediately deleting it, which prevents you from accidentally deleting messages. Whenever you empty the trash or close a database with messages marked for deletion, Notes prompts you for confirmation before deleting the message.

You are not restricted to sending mail messages using Notes Mail; you can use Notes Mail to send any document in any database to any other user of Notes Mail. When you forward a document, a regular mail message appears on-screen with the forwarded document in the body of the memo.

When you first opened Notes, you may have noticed two Address Book databases on your Workspace. The one containing your name is the Personal Address Book, and it is stored on your local hard drive and is empty until you add entries. The other address book is stored on the server and is called the Public Address Book—and that means you can use it but you cannot add entries to it. Whenever you are connected to the server and using Notes, you'll probably want to use the Public Address Book. However, under certain circumstances, you may prefer to use your Personal Address Book. For example, if the Public Address Book contains many entries, you may find it slow to open. Or, if you are not presently connected to the server (it might be down or you might be traveling and not presently connected), the Public Address Book isn't available at all. Your Personal Address Book is always available to you. In this part, you'll learn how to add entries to your Personal Address Book. You'll also learn how to set up a mailing list for groups to whom you regularly send mail.

Viewing Your Mail

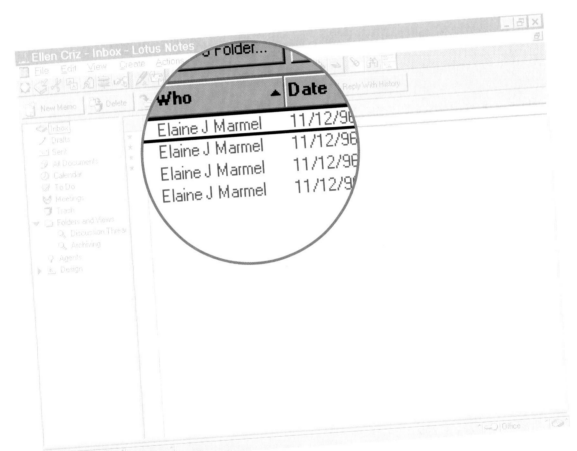

"Why would I do this?"

You must open your Mail database to see mail messages you have received. Once you open your Mail database, you can read, edit, and sort your personal mail messages because all your mail is sent there. This arrangement keeps all the mail you receive in one central location and makes it easier for you to keep track of your mail.

When you open your Mail database, Notes selects, by default, the Inbox in the Navigation pane. The contents of the Inbox appear on the right in the View pane.

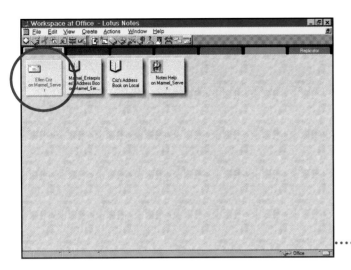

1 Double-click the icon containing an envelope; it probably also contains your name. That's your Mail database icon.

2 Notes displays the Mail database. In the Navigation pane on the left side of the window, you see various views available in the Mail database, such as the Inbox, which is the selected view. The right side of the screen shows you the contents of the selected view, which in the figure, is a list of e-mail messages.

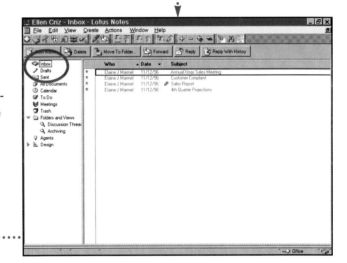

3 To exit from the Mail database, open the **File** menu and choose the **Close** command or press **Esc**. ■

Opening and Closing Mail Messages

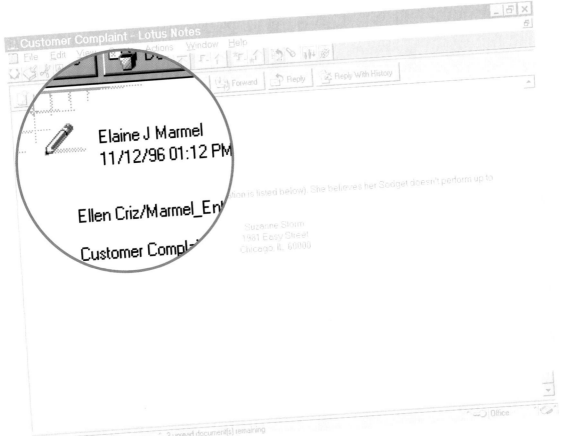

"Why would I do this?"

Without meaning to state the obvious, when you receive mail, you'll probably want to read it; to read a mail message, you open it. Make sure you have your Mail database open.

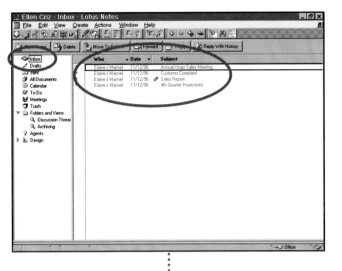

1 Click the **Inbox** in the Navigation pane on the left side of the screen. In the View pane on the right side of the screen, you'll see mail messages waiting for you, who sent them, and the date and subject of each message. Double-click the message you want to read.

2 Notes displays the message on-screen.

> ## Missing Link
>
> A mail message listed in red with a star next to it identifies a message you have not read.

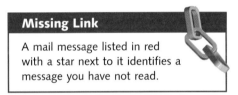

3 When you finish reading the message, close it by opening the **File** menu and choosing the **Close** command. You are returned to the Inbox view. ■

> ## Puzzled?
>
> Notice the star has disappeared from the message you opened. Also, the message is no longer listed in red.

Viewing a Mail Message and an Attached Document

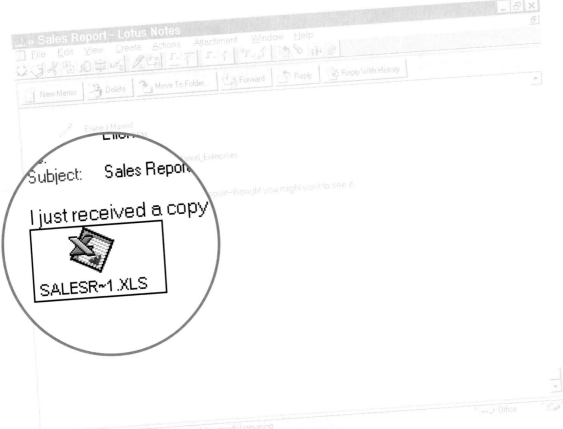

"Why would I do this?"

People can send you documents through Notes by attaching them to a mail message. For any message containing an attached document, you'll see a paper clip next to the subject in the View pane. In this task, you view an attached document.

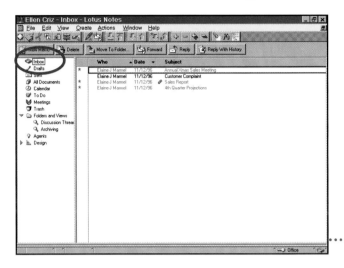

1 Click the Inbox to display incoming messages in the View pane.

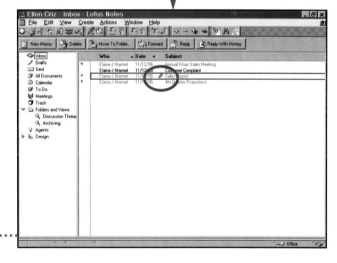

2 Find a document that contains a paper clip next to the subject and double-click it.

3 When Notes displays the document, you see an icon that represents the attached document. Point the mouse at the attachment and press the *right* mouse button.

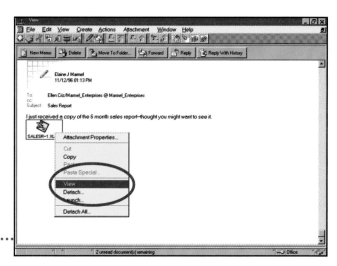

4 A shortcut menu displays. Choose the **View** command.

5 Notes launches a viewer that lets you see, but not change, the contents of the attached document.

Missing Link

If the Viewer doesn't handle the attached document type, it will attempt to launch the application associated with it. You'll learn about launching later in this part.

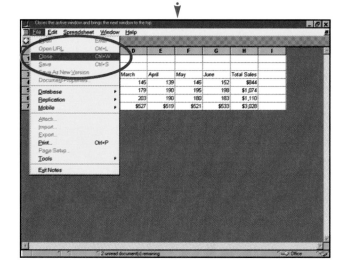

6 To close this window and return to the mail message, open the **File** menu and choose **Close**. ■

Detaching an Attached Document

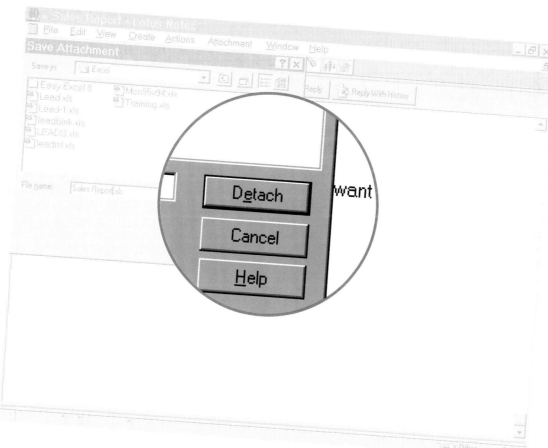

"Why would I do this?"

When you detach a document from a mail message, you save a copy of the document on either your hard drive, a floppy disk, or the server. Detaching doesn't affect either the original document or the attached document. The original document remains with its creator, and the attached document also remains attached to the original mail message.

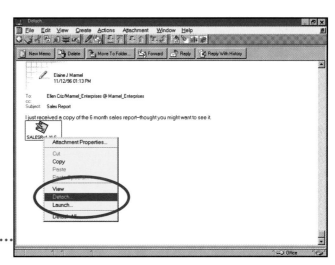

1 In your Mail database, open a mail message that contains a paper clip next to the subject. Point the mouse at the attachment and press the *right* mouse button to display a shortcut menu. Choose the **Detach** command.

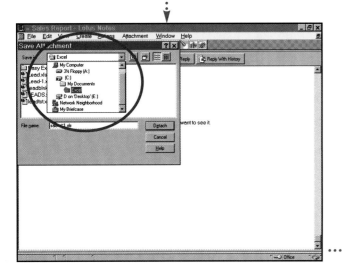

2 Notes displays the Save Attachment dialog box. Click the down arrow next to the Save in list box and choose a location where you want to save the detached copy of the file.

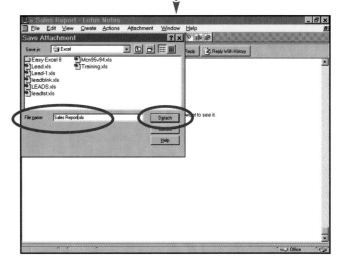

3 Use the File name text box to provide a name for the file. Choose the **Detach** button. Notes saves a copy of the attachment using the name and location you provided and redisplays the mail message. ■

Launching an Attached Document

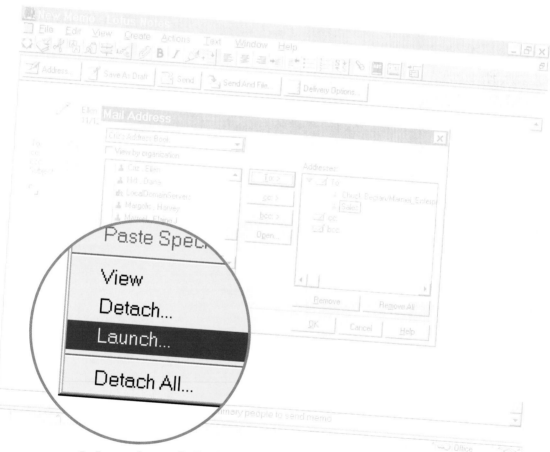

"Why would I do this?"

When you launch an attached document, you open the application that created the document at the same time that you open the document. To launch a document, you must have access, either on your own computer or through the server, to the application that created the attachment. Since launching an application actually opens the document in the application that created it, you can edit the document. Launching differs from viewing in this respect; when you view a document, you cannot edit it.

Task 13: Launching an Attached Document

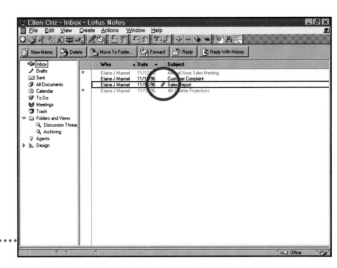

1 In your Mail database, open a mail message that contains a paper clip next to the subject.

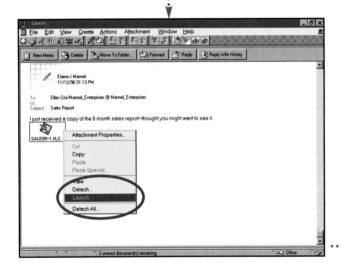

2 Point the mouse at the attachment and press the *right* mouse button to display a shortcut menu. Choose the **Launch** command.

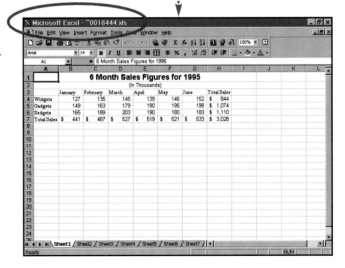

3 The attached document opens in the application that created it. ■

Puzzled?

When you finish working with the document, use the application's **Exit** command to close the application. You'll return to the Notes mail message containing the attached document.

Printing a Mail Message

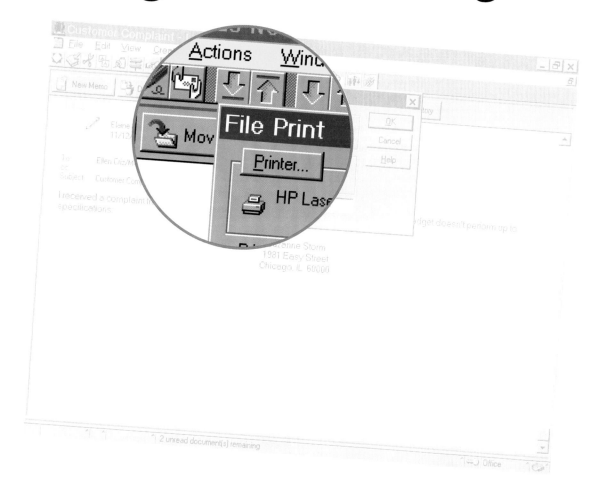

"Why would I do this?"

You may want to print a copy of a mail message. Printing a mail message in Notes is similar to printing a document in other applications.

1 In your Mail database, open the message you want to print.

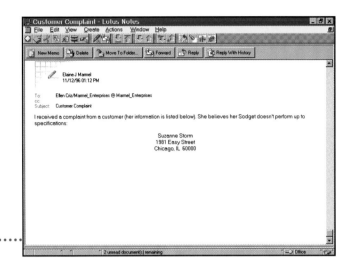

2 Open the **File** menu and choose the **Print** command.

Puzzled?

If your printer supports graphics, you'll see virtually the same image on paper that you see on-screen.

3 Notes displays the File Print dialog box. When you choose **OK**, the mail message prints. ■

Missing Link

If you print a document that contains an attachment, you'll see a placeholder for the attachment in the printed message that looks just like the graphic you see on-screen.

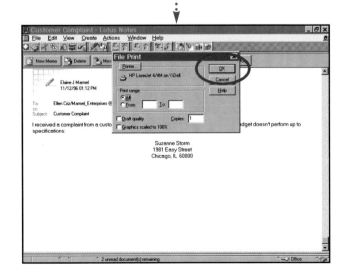

Organizing Your Mail Messages

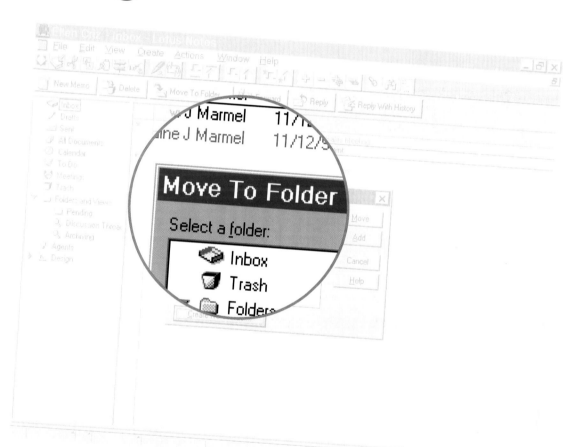

"Why would I do this?"

After a while, you may start to accumulate many mail messages in your Mail database. Although you can delete those you no longer need, you may want to save some messages for future reference. You can organize your mail messages by placing them into folders. You can

also move messages in the Sent view, the All Documents view, the To Do view, the Trash view, and the Discussion Thread view.

In this lesson, you create a new folder to store messages and move a mail message to that folder.

43

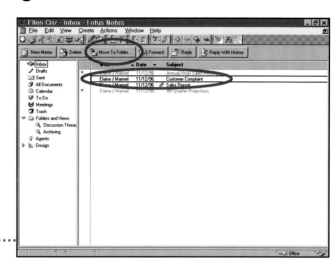

1 In the Inbox, highlight the message you want to move and click the **Move To Folder** button.

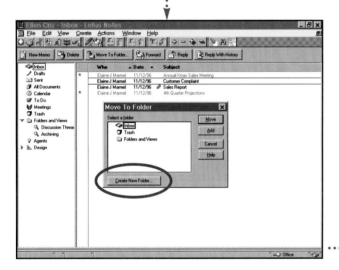

2 Notes displays the Move To Folder dialog box. (If the folder you want to place the message in already exists, skip to Step 5.) Choose the **Create New Folder** button to create a new folder.

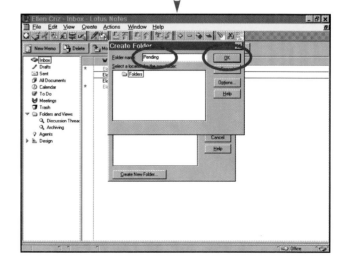

3 Notes displays the Create Folder dialog box. In the Folder name text box, type a name for the new folder (I created "Pending") and choose **OK**.

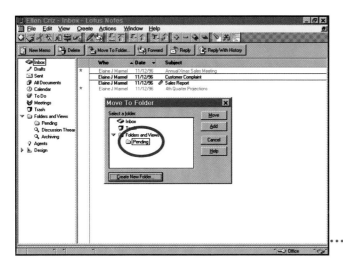

4 Notes redisplays the Move To Folder dialog box, and the new folder you just created is selected.

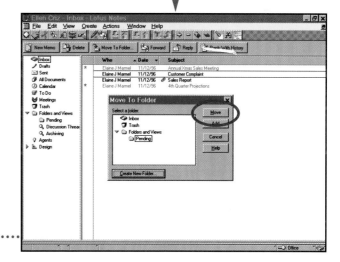

5 If necessary, highlight the folder in which you want to store the message and choose **Move**.

6 Notes closes the dialog box. The message disappears from the Inbox, but when you click the folder where the message is located, it appears in the folder where you moved it. ■

Missing Link

You can move messages to folders while the message is open and you're reading it. Just open the message and complete Steps 2–5.

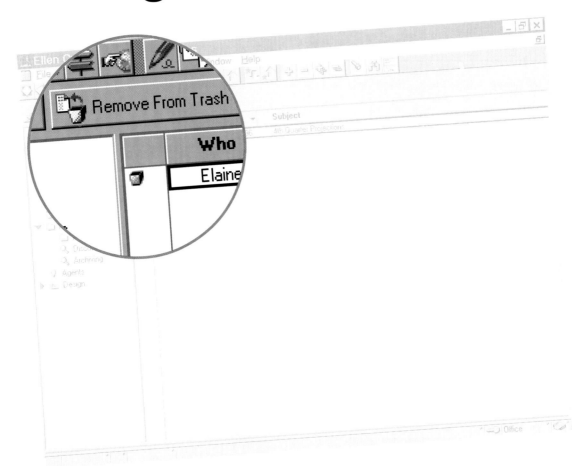

Deleting Mail

"Why would I do this?"

You can delete mail messages you no longer need in two ways: either while you read the message or from one of the views where you see the message. Regardless of which method you use, you initially mark messages for deletion; in the View pane, you'll see a trash can icon appear next to a marked message. After marking for deletion, you must take a second action

to actually delete the messages you marked: you must refresh the view.

If you accidentally mark the wrong message for deletion, you can "undelete" the message before you refresh the view. Simply repeat the action you took to delete the message, and Notes will unmark the message.

46

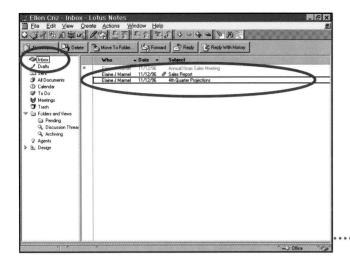

1 Open the Mail database and select the view containing messages you want to delete. Highlight the message you want to delete.

2 Click the **Delete** button. Notes marks the message for deletion by displaying a trash can next to the message. Repeat this step for each message you want to delete. Select the Trash view.

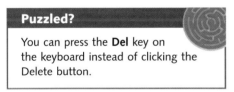

Puzzled?

You can press the **Del** key on the keyboard instead of clicking the Delete button.

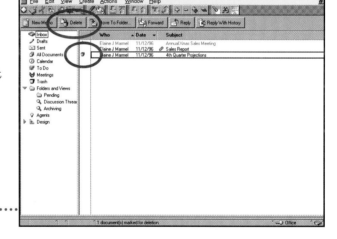

3 The messages you have marked for deletion appear in the View pane. Click the **Empty Trash** button to delete all documents, or highlight a particular document and click the **Remove From Trash** button to leave the document in its original view. ■

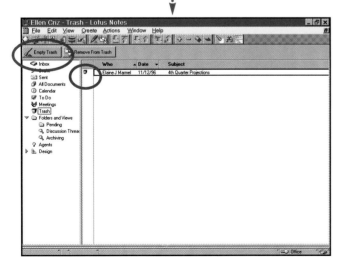

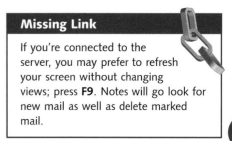

Missing Link

If you're connected to the server, you may prefer to refresh your screen without changing views; press **F9**. Notes will go look for new mail as well as delete marked mail.

TASK 17

Replying to a Message

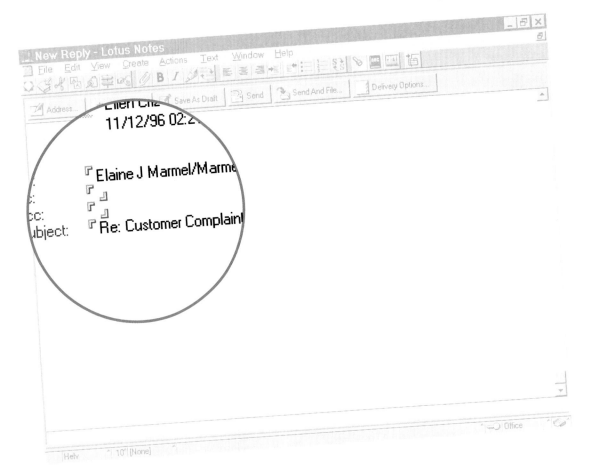

"Why would I do this?"

"Mail" usually implies a two-way correspondence. While you aren't required to answer mail messages, you'll have many occasions where you want to respond to the sender. In Notes, you use the Reply feature to answer a message.

If you receive a response to a message you sent and you open the response, you'll see an icon

next to the subject that represents the original message. You can double-click that icon to open your original message. And, if you really want to be considerate of the person to whom you are replying, you can include a copy of the original message in your reply.

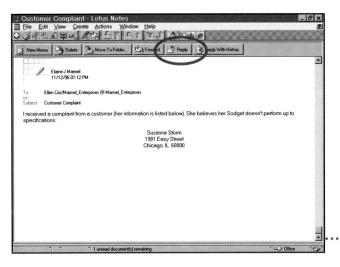

1 In your Mail database, open the message to which you want to reply. Click the **Reply** button.

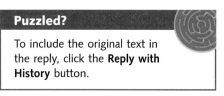

Puzzled?

To include the original text in the reply, click the **Reply with History** button.

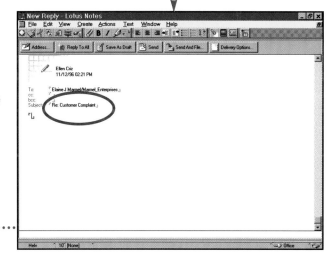

2 Notes opens a new screen that contains the address of the person who originally sent you the message and the subject of the message.

3 Fill in the message and click the **Send** button. ■

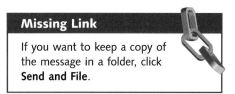

Missing Link

If you want to keep a copy of the message in a folder, click **Send and File**.

TASK

18

Forwarding a Message

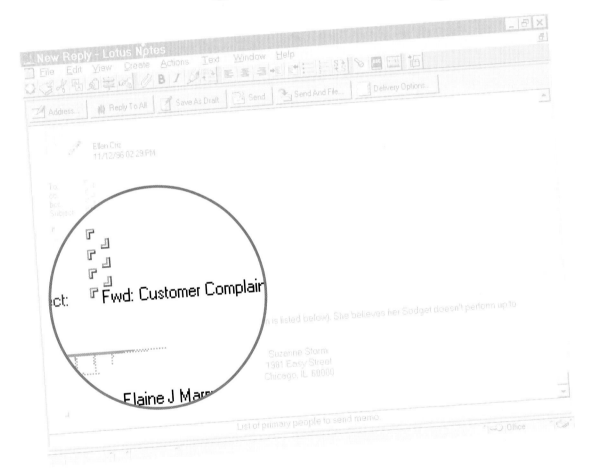

"Why would I do this?"

You may receive a mail message that you want to pass along to someone else. In Notes, you forward the message. You can forward any message in any database to another Notes user. And you can forward the message while reading it or from any of the following views: the Inbox view, the Sent view, the All Documents view, the

Discussion Thread view, and any of the folders you create.

When you forward a message, Notes creates a mail message where the top portion of the screen shows you as the sender, and the bottom portion of the screen shows the message that you are forwarding and who sent the message to you.

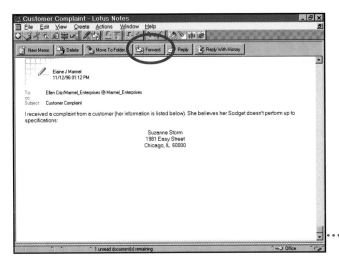

1 In your Mail database, open the message you want to forward. Click the **Forward** button.

Missing Link

You can also forward messages without opening them; select a view, highlight the message you want to forward, and click the **Forward** button.

2 Notes redraws your screen and creates a copy of the message, waiting for you to supply a recipient.

Puzzled?

If you're unsure about addressing a message, use the Address Book. You'll learn more about it in the next task.

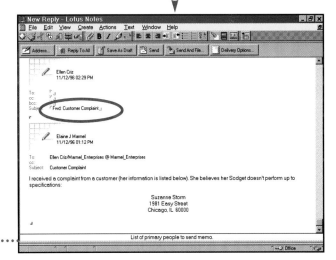

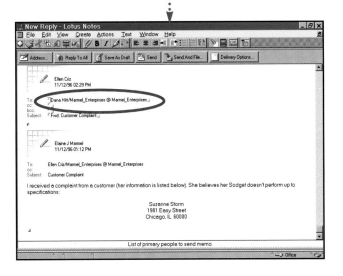

3 Type the recipient's address in the To field. Be sure to include her mail address, her server, and her domain name. The mail address and server name are separated by the forward slash (/), and the server name is separated from the domain name by an at sign (@). Click the **Send** button to forward the message. Notes sends the message and redisplays the original. ■

Missing Link

If Notes recognizes the name you're typing, Notes will attempt to automatically complete the address for you.

TASK

19

Adding Entries to Your Address Book

"Why would I do this?"

Addressing mail is much easier if you use an Address Book. When you first opened Notes, you may have noticed two Address Book databases on your Workspace. The one containing your name is the Personal Address Book, and it is stored on your local hard drive. The other address book is stored on the server and is called the Public Address Book—and that means you can use it but you cannot add entries

to it. When connected to the server and using Notes, you'll probably want to use the Public Address Book. However, under certain circumstances, you may prefer to use your Personal Address Book. For example, you can always store addresses in your Personal Address Book.

In this task, you'll learn how to copy addresses from the Public Address Book.

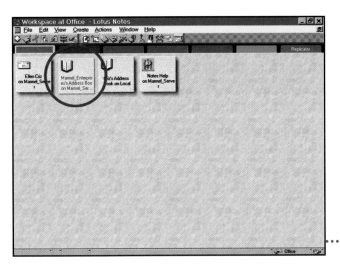

1 From the Workspace, open the **Public Address Book** database. It's the Address Book icon that doesn't contain your name.

2 Highlight the name of the person whose address information you want to place in your Personal Address Book database, and click **Copy to Personal Address Book**.

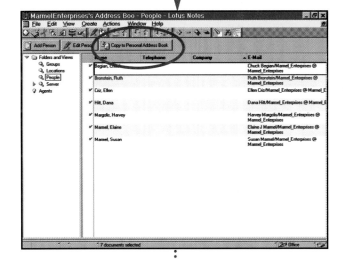

Missing Link

Copy multiple addresses simultaneously by selecting several names. Highlight a name and click or press the **Spacebar**; you'll see a check next to the name. Repeat this action to select additional names.

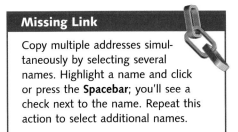

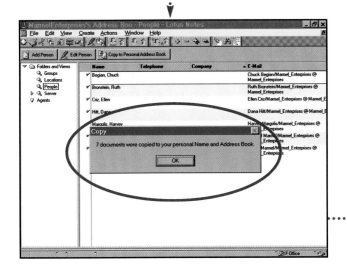

3 Notes displays the message that documents were copied to your personal Address Book; the number of documents copied depends on the number of selections you made in Step 2. Choose **OK**.

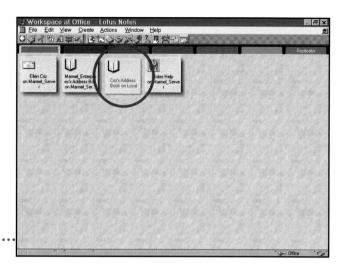

4 Open the **File** menu and choose the **Close** command to close the server's Address Book database and return to the workspace. Open your local Address Book database—the one with your name on it.

5 You'll see the name(s) and address(es) you copied in the People view of your Personal Address Book. Highlight a name and click the **Edit Person** button.

Missing Link

To manually add a person to your local Address Book database, open that database, click **Add Person**, and fill out the Person document.

6 Notes displays a Person document; you can use this document as a model if you want to manually add a person to your local Address Book database. Fill in the First Name, Last Name, Full User Name and Mail Domain. You'll only need to complete this document if you're adding someone to your Personal Address Book who isn't entered in the Public Address Book. ■

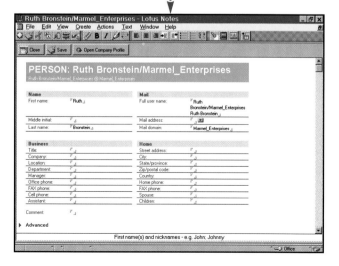

Creating a New Message

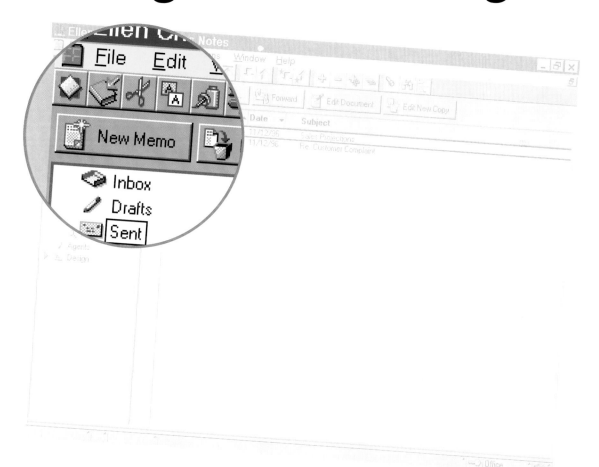

"Why would I do this?"

Now that you have some people in your Address Book, you'll find it easy to send them mail. Creating a new mail message is, in many ways, similar to forwarding and replying to mail. And when you send a message, you have several delivery options from which to choose; they appear at the end of this task.

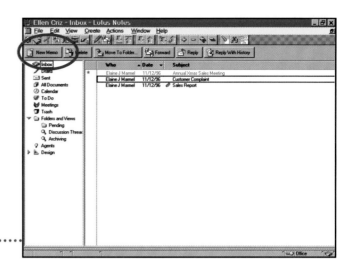

1 In your Mail database, click the **New Memo** button.

2 Notes displays a new memo ready for you to complete. Notice the insertion point is already located between the brackets in the To: field.

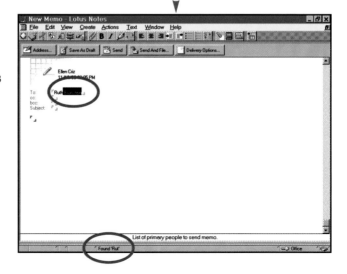

3 To use Quick Addressing, type a few letters of the person's first or last name; when Notes finds the name, you'll see a message in the status bar at the bottom of the screen. Press **Enter** to finish filling in the address.

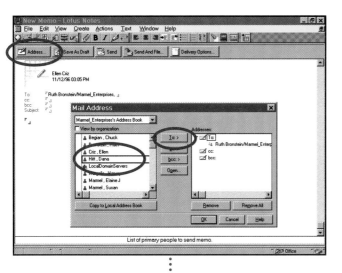

4 Let's add another recipient using the Address Book. Click the **Address** button on the Action bar. The Mail Address dialog box appears. From the list on the left, select the person to whom you want to send the mail. Then, click the **To:>** button.

Missing Link

Use the list box at the top of the Mail Address dialog box to switch between your Personal Address Book and the Public Address Book.

5 The names you choose are displayed in the Addresses: list on the right. When you have finished choosing the people to whom you want to send your message, choose **OK**.

Missing Link

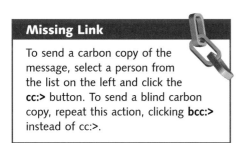

To send a carbon copy of the message, select a person from the list on the left and click the **cc:>** button. To send a blind carbon copy, repeat this action, clicking **bcc:>** instead of cc:>.

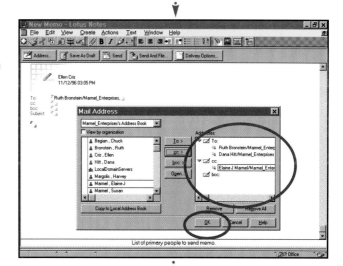

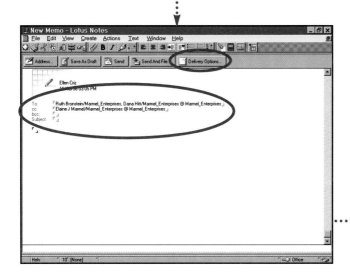

6 Notes fills in the address portion of the new mail message. Fill in the subject line and the message. Then, click the **Delivery Options** button.

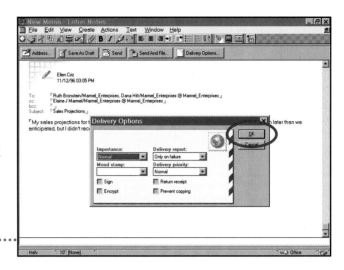

7 See the table at the end of this task for an explanation of the Delivery options. Select your Delivery options and choose **OK**. Notes redisplays your message. Click **Send** to close and send the message.

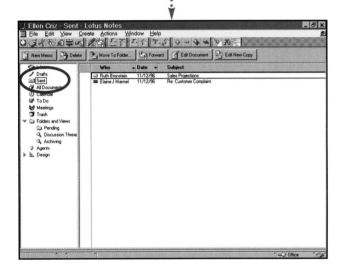

8 Click the **Sent** view to see your message. A red envelope will appear if you set an importance other than Normal. A yellow envelope will appear if you didn't change the message's importance. ▩

Delivery Option	Description
Importance	Displays an icon to the recipient that illustrates how important the memo is.
Mood stamp	Personalize the message with options such as **Personal**, **Confidential**, **Private**, and **Thank You**.
Delivery report	Requests a confirmation that Notes has delivered your message. **Only on Failure** sends a report only if the server failed to deliver the message; **Confirm Delivery** sends a message confirming delivery or reporting failure; **Trace Entire Path** sends reports from every server through which the message is routed.
Delivery priority	**High** routes the message immediately; **Normal** routes the message the next time the server is scheduled to send mail; **Low** routes the message during off-peak hours, usually between midnight and 6 a.m.
Sign	Incorporates a digital signature in your message, assuring the recipient that you are, indeed, the person who sent the message.
Encrypt	Makes a message readable to the recipient only.
Return receipt	Requests a confirmation that your message has been read by the recipient.
Prevent copying	Sends a message that the recipient cannot forward.

Attaching a Document to a Mail Message

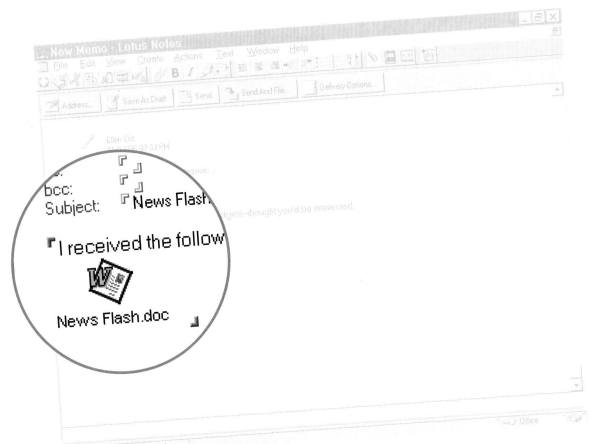

"Why would I do this?"

You may want to send a document you created outside Notes in another program to someone else using Notes Mail. To send a document, you attach the document to a mail message. You must create or have access to the document

you want to attach before you start the mail message. In this task, you learn how to attach a News Flash already created in Microsoft Word.

As a side note, to send a Notes document to someone else, you forward it. You attach only documents created outside Notes.

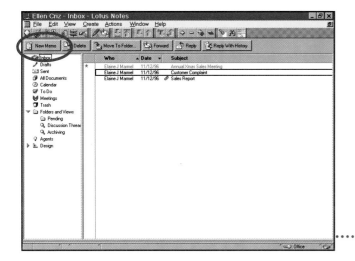

1 In your Mail database, click the **New Memo** button.

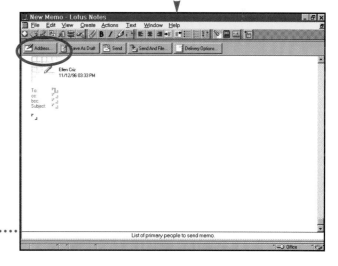

2 Notes displays a new memo ready for you to complete.

3 Provide an addressee.

Missing Link

Either click the **Address** button to use the Address Book or type a few letters of the person's name to use the Quick Addressing feature.

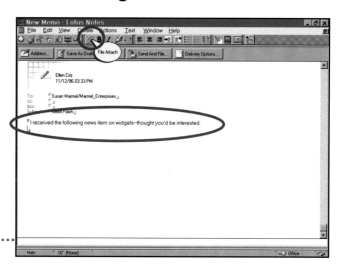

4 Complete the subject and type any text you want to include in the mail message. Optionally, press **Enter** to start a new line before attaching the document. Click the **File Attach** SmartIcon.

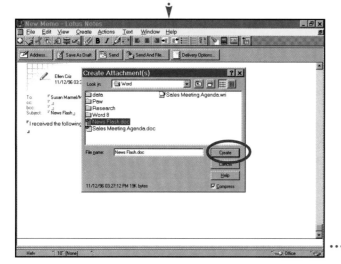

5 Notes displays the Create Attachment(s) dialog box. Navigate to the folder containing the document you want to attach, highlight the document, and choose **Create**.

6 Notes inserts an attachment icon in your message. The icon you see depends on the type of document you chose to attach. ■

Creating a Mailing List

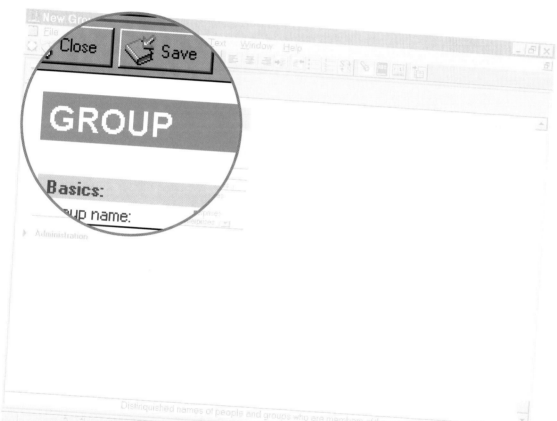

"Why would I do this?"

You may find that you regularly send mail to the same group of people. Instead of selecting them individually each time you need to send them mail, you can create a mailing list that includes them. Notes stores the mailing list in your Personal Address Book database, and when you need to send mail to the group, you can simply select the list. Notes will then send the message you create to each person included

in the list. Note: the Public Address Book may contain some predefined mailing lists that you can use but *not* modify.

When you create a mailing list, you provide a name for the list. You'll find it most useful to use a name that describes the group or its purpose. For example, you could name the group Sales if the group contains members of the Sales department.

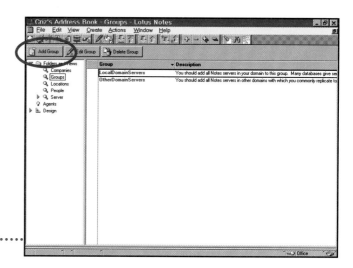

1 Open your Personal Address Book (the one containing your name) and, in the Navigation pane, click **Groups**. Click the **Add Group** button.

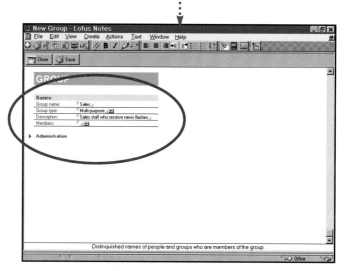

2 Notes displays a Group document. By default, the insertion point appears between the brackets in the Group name: field. Type the name you want to use when addressing the group.

3 Leave the Group type as Multi-purpose and supply, if you want, a description of the group. Click the down arrow next to Members.

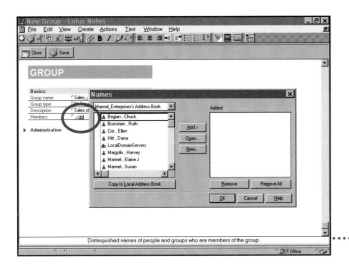

4 Notes opens the Names dialog box.

5 From the list box on the left side of the Names dialog box, highlight a name and click **Add>**. Repeat this action to add each person you want to include in the Group. Click **OK**.

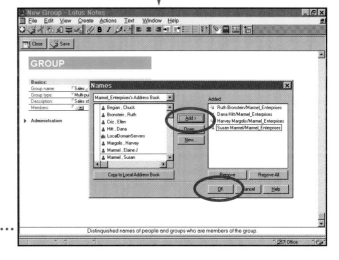

6 Notes inserts the names into the Group document.

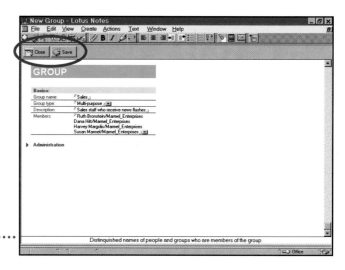

7 Click the **Save** button on the Action bar to save the document. Click the **Close** button.

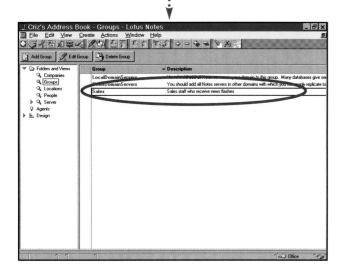

8 Notes redisplays your Personal Address Book, and you can see your mailing list whenever you select Group from the Navigation pane. ■

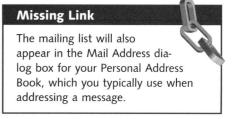

Missing Link

The mailing list will also appear in the Mail Address dialog box for your Personal Address Book, which you typically use when addressing a message.

Sending Mail to a Group of People

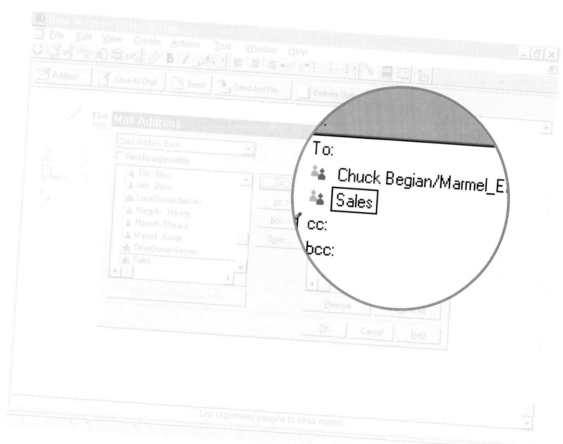

"Why would I do this?"

You can easily send the same mail message to a group of people. You can address the message to more than one person, or you can use the mailing list you created in the last task to send the message.

1 In your Mail database, click the **New Memo** button to start creating a new mail message. Click the **Address** button to open the Mail Address dialog box.

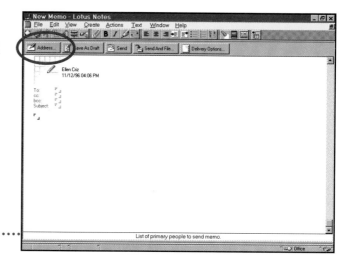

Missing Link

To switch between your Personal Address Book and the Public Address Book, use the list box at the top of the Mail Address dialog box.

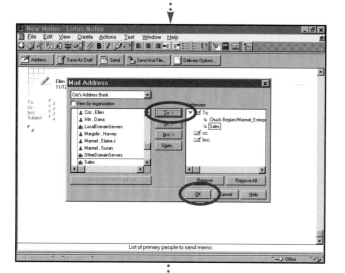

2 Highlight the first name to whom you want to send the message and click the **To:>** button. Repeat this action for each person to whom you want to send the message. Choose **OK**.

Missing Link

To use your mailing list, make sure you are viewing your Personal Address Book. Then, highlight the mailing list and click the **To:>** button. To see who is in the mailing list, click the **Open** button. After viewing the mailing list, click **Close**.

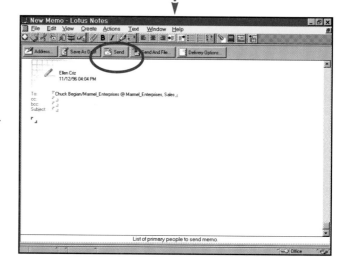

3 The name of each person you selected appears in the To section of your mail message, and Notes will deliver a copy of the message to each of them when you click **Send**. ■

PART III

Letting Notes Help Plan and Manage Your Time

THE NEWEST FEATURE ADDED to Notes 4.5 helps you schedule and manage your time. The Calendar in Notes is a view available from the Navigation pane in the Mail database, and you can view the Calendar in several formats. Initially, you'll see one week at a time, but you'll learn how to switch to view the Calendar two days at a time, two weeks at a time, or one month at a time.

You can use the Calendar view to schedule five different types of entries: reminders, appointments, events, anniversaries, and invitations to meetings. For any of these Calendar entries, you'll have space to type a brief description of the entry as well as additional space for a detailed description. If the description you type in the Brief Description text box exceeds what Notes can display in your Calendar, Notes will attempt to display the entire brief description when you use the mouse to point at the entry on the Calendar.

Reminders are just what you think they are: entries you can place on your Calendar to remind you of some occasion. Reminders differ from appointments in that reminders occur at only one specific time while appointments are entries that span a time range—say from 3:30 p.m. to 4:30 p.m.—and last less than one day. Events are entries that can span more than one day. Anniversaries are entries that last all day and occur at regular intervals—like birthdays or the weekly staff meeting you attend. Invitations to meetings record meetings you set up—if you have access to the calendars of those you invite, Notes will even help you find a time that's convenient for everyone. Notes also lets you track the responses to your meeting invitations, and in the new Meetings view, you'll see invitations and responses grouped together.

While you can repeat any type of Calendar entry, you'll learn how to repeat an entry in the task where you create an anniversary; after all, logically, anniversaries occur every "so often." You also can set an alarm for any kind of entry; you'll learn how to set an alarm when you create an appointment.

One of the best organization techniques available is the To Do list, on which you place and prioritize tasks you need to accomplish. The tasks that might appear on a To Do list are not necessarily date-dependent; sometimes, you just need to make a list of things you need to do and then order them by their importance. The To Do list view in Notes is particularly useful because you can optionally choose to display a task in your Calendar. You also can assign tasks on the To Do list to other people (personally, I think that's my favorite feature). The To Do view displays tasks you create and messages you receive that ask you to respond by a specified date. By default, items in the To Do view appear in one of four categories:

- Overdue—Items with due dates prior to today.

- Current—Items with due dates of today or later and either no start dates or start dates of today or earlier.

- Future—Items with start dates and due dates after today.

- Completed—Items completed, regardless of start or due date.

You may also see a "Rejected" category, which shows tasks you assigned to others that they rejected as well as tasks others assigned to you that you rejected.

Within each category, tasks appear in the To Do view in order of priority. As time goes by and deadline dates pass, tasks move from one category to another—but not automatically. Periodically, you'll want to update the To Do view to ensure that tasks appear in the correct category. In addition, as you complete tasks, you will want to mark them completed to achieve that all-important sense of accomplishment. Mail messages you receive that ask you to "do something" by a specified date will also appear on your To Do list; since you can't "complete" mail messages, you'll learn to remove them from the To Do view—and removing an item from the To Do view doesn't affect any other view in your Mail database.

Notes contains two schedule-related profiles you set up to describe how Notes should behave: the Calendar Profile and the Delegation Profile. As you saw in Part II, Notes 4.5 won't even let you create a new mail message without setting a Calendar Profile. Using the Calendar Profile, you can change such items as the default type of Calendar entry Notes displays when you create an entry. You also can enable alarms and conflict checking. If you enable alarms, Notes can warn you when various Calendar entries you create are about to occur. If you enable conflict checking, you can tell Notes to check your Calendar for conflicts with other entries when you schedule appointments, meetings, anniversaries, or events. The Delegation Profile specifies who besides you has access to your Calendar and what actions those accessing your Calendar can take.

24

Setting the Calendar Profile

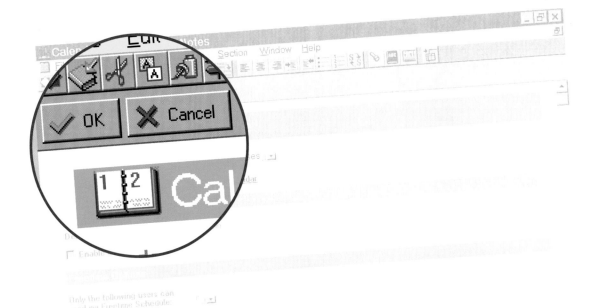

"Why would I do this?"

In the last section, when you first opened your Mail database and tried to create e-mail, you saw a message from Notes saying you needed to set a Calendar Profile. At that time, you just accepted the defaults Notes suggested. But, you may want to change the profile to change the default type of Calendar entry Notes displays when you create an entry. Or, you might want to enable alarms or conflict checking. If you enable alarms, you'll be able to add an alarm to entries you create and have Notes warn you when various Calendar entries are about to occur. If you enable conflict checking, you can tell Notes to check for conflicts whenever you schedule any

type of Calendar event except a reminder. If Notes finds a conflict, you'll see a warning; if you want, you can ignore the warning and schedule the appointment anyway.

Although you can set your Calendar Profile from the Notes Workspace, we'll work from your Mail database, since that's the place where you'll use the Calendar. If necessary, double-click the Mail database icon to open your Mail database. If you've just started Notes for the first time today, you'll need to provide your password.

■▲●■▲●■▲●■▲●■

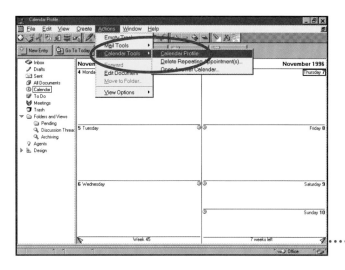

1 Open the **Actions** menu and choose the **Calendar Tools** command. From the cascading menu that appears, choose **Calendar Profile**.

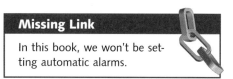

Missing Link

In this book, we won't be setting automatic alarms.

2 In the Calendar Profile window, you can set Scheduling Options, Freetime Options, and Advanced Calendar Options.

Puzzled?

You need to scroll down to see the Advanced Calendar Options, as you'll see in a minute.

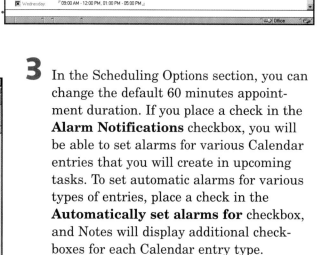

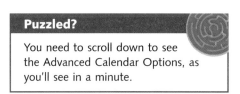

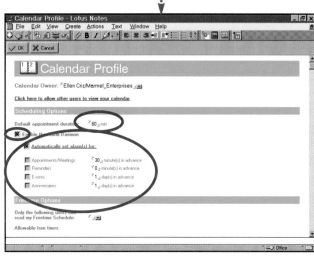

3 In the Scheduling Options section, you can change the default 60 minutes appointment duration. If you place a check in the **Alarm Notifications** checkbox, you will be able to set alarms for various Calendar entries that you will create in upcoming tasks. To set automatic alarms for various types of entries, place a check in the **Automatically set alarms for** checkbox, and Notes will display additional checkboxes for each Calendar entry type.

4 In the Freetime Options section, use the list box button at the top of the section to select other users who can read your Freetime Schedule.

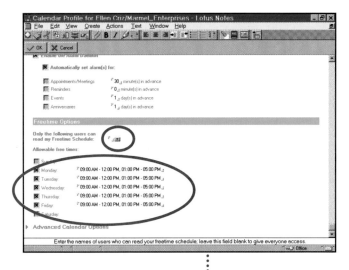

Missing Link

When you select users who can read your Freetime Schedule, Notes displays the Names dialog box, which lets you choose an address book to view. You highlight a person or group and click the **Add** button. When you finish, click **OK** to redisplay the Calendar Profile window.

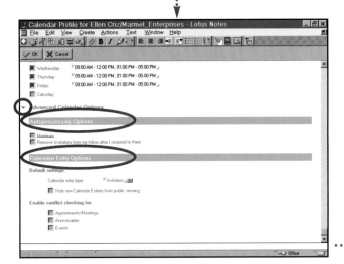

5 Click **Advanced Calendar Options** to display Autoprocessing Options and Calendar Entry Options.

Missing Link

If you "autoprocess" meetings, Notes lets you specify users from whom you will automatically accept meetings. In Calendar Entry Options, you can change the default entry type.

6 Place a check in each checkbox to tell Notes to check for conflicts for all available types of events; when you create an entry, Notes will then look for conflicts and display a dialog box that warns you if Notes finds a conflict. Click **OK** to save your Calendar Profile and redisplay the Mail database window. ■

Missing Link

Notes considers *any* type of Calendar event except Reminders a potential conflict for any *other* type of Calendar event.

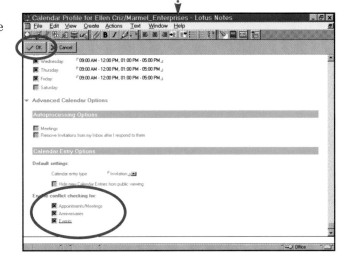

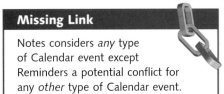

Deciding Who Uses Your Calendar

"Why would I do this?"

In the previous task, you set the options for how your Calendar will function. You may have noticed that you can give other people access to your Calendar. You use your Delegation Profile to decide who can read your Calendar and who can make entries on your Calendar. As you'll learn in Part VI, the Delegation Profile also defines who has access to your e-mail, which is particularly useful if you travel without a computer.

Although you can set your Delegation Profile from the Notes Workspace, we'll work from your Mail database, since that's the place where you'll use the Calendar. If necessary, double-click the **Mail** database icon to open your Mail database. If you've just started Notes for the first time today, you'll need to provide your password.

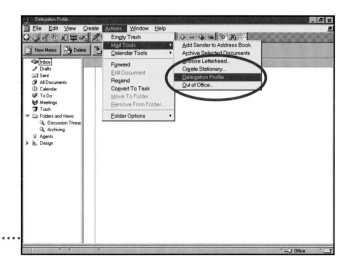

1 Open the **Actions** menu and choose **Mail Tools**. From the cascading menu, choose **Delegation Profile**.

2 Use the Calendar Access section to determine who can read your Calendar and who can make changes to your Calendar.

3 If you choose either list box button in the Calendar Access section, Notes displays the Names dialog box that you can use to choose an Address Book and people. Highlight a person's name on the left side of the box and click the **Add** button. Then, click **OK** to redisplay the Delegation Profile window, and click **OK** again to save the Delegation Profile. ■

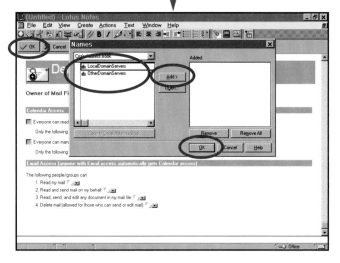

Viewing the Calendar

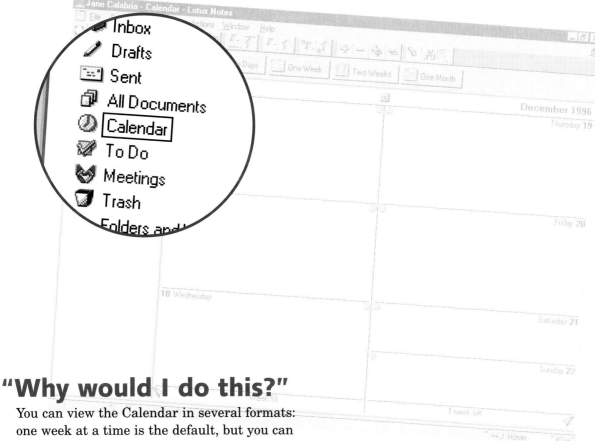

"Why would I do this?"

You can view the Calendar in several formats: one week at a time is the default, but you can switch to two days at a time, two weeks at a time, or one month at a time. Today's date always appears in red, but you click other dates to select them. If you need to select a date that you can't see, you can switch to a different view to select the date, or you can stay in the same view and move to the date.

As you'll see in this task, appointment times don't appear by default in some Calendar formats, but you can easily view appointment times.

Task 26: Viewing the Calendar

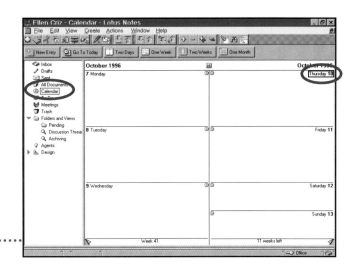

1 Click the **Calendar** view in the Navigation pane. Notes displays the Calendar; by default, you see one week at a time. Today's date appears in red and is selected—notice the black outline that appears around today's date.

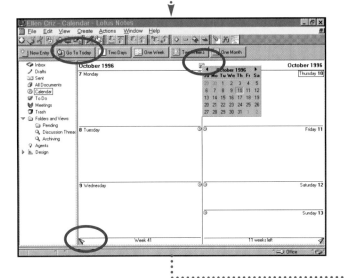

2 To select another day, click that date, such as November 8. To select a date you can't see, click the curls at the bottom of the Calendar pages to "turn the page" until you see the date you want to click, or click the date icon at the top of the Calendar to display a small, month-view Calendar from which you can select the date.

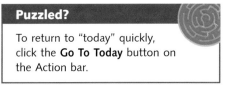

Puzzled?

To return to "today" quickly, click the **Go To Today** button on the Action bar.

3 To display one month at one time, click the **One Month** button on the Action bar.

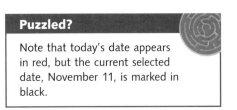

Puzzled?

Note that today's date appears in red, but the current selected date, November 11, is marked in black.

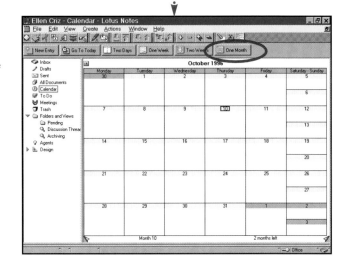

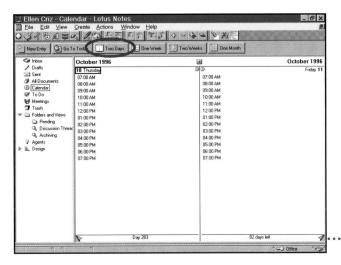

4 To display only two days at one time, click the **Two Days** button on the Action bar.

Missing Link

The Two Day view is the only one which displays the times by default.

5 To display two weeks at one time, click the **Two Weeks** button on the Action bar.

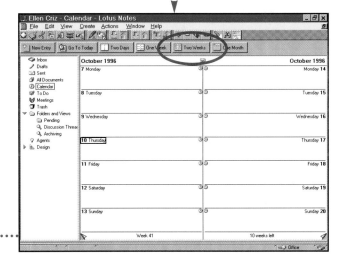

6 To see appointment times for a particular day, click the small clock on that day. Then use the arrows underneath the clock to scroll the appointment times up or down. To hide appointment times, click the small clock again. ■

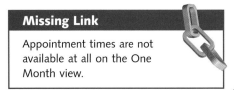

Missing Link

Appointment times are not available at all on the One Month view.

79

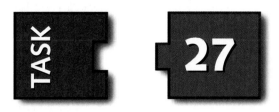

TASK 27

Storing a Reminder

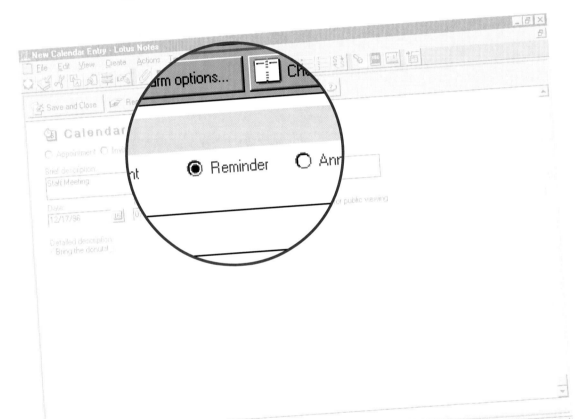

"Why would I do this?"

Suppose you have an upcoming deadline and you want to remind yourself about the deadline before it occurs. You can use Notes' Reminder Calendar entry to place an entry on the Calendar. The entry on your Calendar will be associated with a specific date and time.

You can create reminders without first selecting either a date or time, but you might find that filling out the Calendar Entry document goes

faster if you do select at least the date before you create the reminder. You'll have space to type a brief description of the appointment as well as additional space for a detailed description.

Task 27: Storing a Reminder

1 In the Calendar view, select the date on which you want to store the reminder. To save time, you can display times on the Calendar and click the time at which you want the reminder to appear. Then, click the **New Entry** button on the Action bar.

> **Puzzled?**
>
> Instead of clicking the **New Entry** button, you can double-click the time you selected. Alternatively, you don't need to display times; Notes will let you set the time in the Calendar Entry window.

2 On the Calendar Entry document, click the **Reminder** option button. Fill in a brief description using less than 100 characters. If necessary, change the date and time. Use the Detailed Description text box to add information. Click the **Save and Close** button in the Action bar to save the reminder.

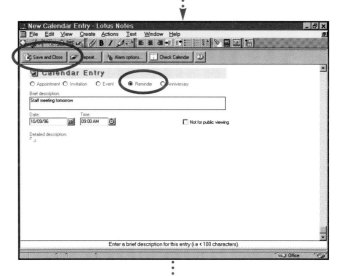

> **Missing Link**
>
> Notes doesn't check for conflicts with Reminders, so the **Pencil In** checkbox has no effect. Use the **Not for Public Viewing** checkbox to hide the reminder when others are checking your Calendar.

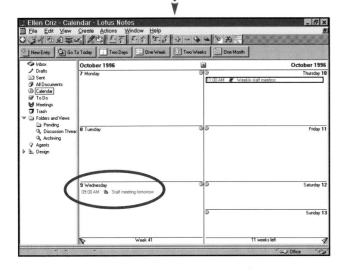

3 Even if you click the clock on the date of the appointment and hide appointment times, Notes will still display the reminder you just created. ■

> **Missing Link**
>
> To edit a reminder, double-click it to open it. Then, click the **Edit Document** button on the Action bar. Make your changes and choose **Save and Close**.

Creating an Appointment

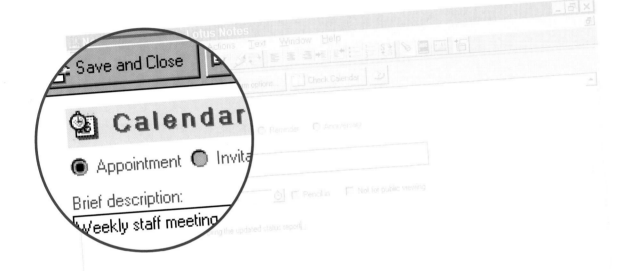

"Why would I do this?"

Appointments appear on the Calendar view of your Mail database on the date and at the time you specify. If you set your Calendar Preferences so that Notes checks for conflicts, then you won't need to worry—as you schedule an appointment, Notes will check the rest of your Calendar entries and display a warning if any entries conflict with the appointment you're trying to schedule. If you want, you can ignore the warning and schedule the appointment anyway.

You can set an alarm for any type of Calendar entry. If you're like me and you get caught up in other projects you're working on, alarms make particular sense when setting an appointment because then you can let Notes warn you of the upcoming appointment.

As with reminders, you can create appointments without first selecting either the date or the time, but you might find that filling out the Calendar Entry document goes faster if you select the date and time before you create the appointment.

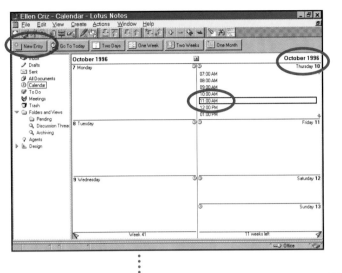

1 In the Calendar view, select the date on which you want to schedule the appointment. To save time, you can display appointment times and click the time you want for the appointment. Then, click the **New Entry** button on the Action bar.

Puzzled?

Instead of clicking the New Entry button, you can double-click the appointment time.

2 On the Calendar Entry document, click the **Appointment** option button. Fill in a brief description using less than 100 characters. If necessary, change the appointment date and time. Use the Detailed Description text box to add information. Click the **Alarm Options** button to set an alarm that warns you about the appointment.

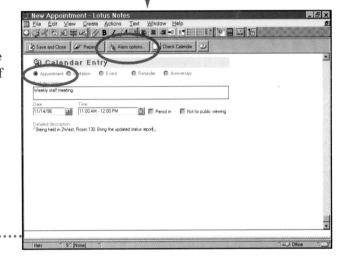

3 Choose the **Before** option button to set the alarm to occur before the appointment. Use the Minutes box to specify when the alarm should appear. In the **Alarm Message** text box, type the message you want to see when the alarm goes off. Choose **OK** to redisplay the Calendar Entry document. Click the **Save and Close** button in the Action bar to save the appointment.

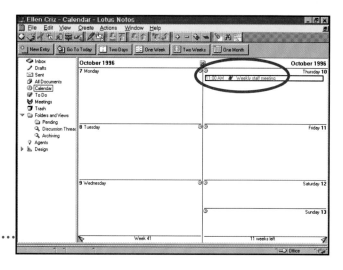

4 Even if you click the clock on the date of the appointment to hide appointment times, Notes will still display the appointment you just created.

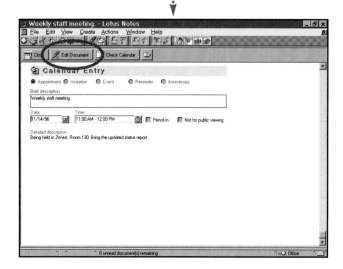

5 To edit an appointment, double-click it to open it. Then, click the **Edit Document** button on the Action bar. Notes redisplays the Calendar Entry document so that you can make your changes and choose **Save and Close**. ■

Missing Link

If you choose the **On** option button, Notes lets you set both a date and a time for the alarm. When you set an alarm for a reminder, you won't see any option buttons, but the Set Alarm dialog box looks like you chose the **On** option button.

Recording an Event

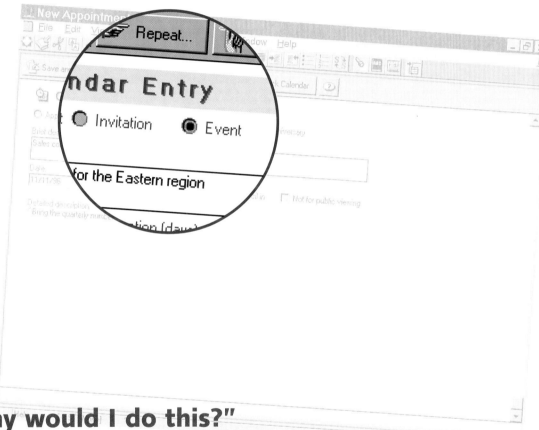

"Why would I do this?"

Events are very similar to appointments and reminders except that typically, they span more than one day. Therefore, you set only a date for an event; you don't set a time. Events are particularly useful for conferences you attend or trips out of town.

Like reminders and appointments, you can create events without first selecting a date, but again, you might find that filling out the Calendar Entry document goes faster if you select the beginning date before you create the event.

1 In the Calendar view, select the date on which the event begins. Then, click the **New Entry** button on the Action bar.

Puzzled?

Instead of clicking the New Entry button, you can double-click the date you selected.

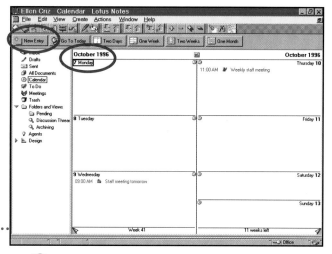

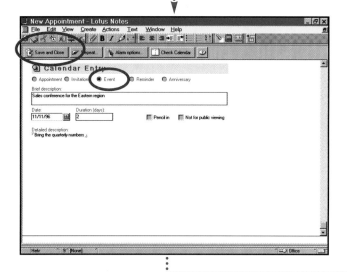

2 On the Calendar Entry document, click the **Event** option button. Fill in a brief description. If necessary, change the date. Fill in a duration, in days, for the event. Use the Detailed Description text box to add information. Click the **Save and Close** button in the Action bar to save the reminder.

Missing Link

Use the **Pencil in** checkbox for events that aren't certain; Notes will ignore these entries while checking for conflicts. Use the **Not for Public Viewing** checkbox to hide the appointment when others are checking your Calendar for free time.

3 Notes will display the events beginning on the date you selected and on all subsequent dates, based on the duration you supplied. ■

Missing Link

To edit an event, double-click it to open it. Then, click the **Edit Document** button on the Action bar. Make your changes and choose **Save and Close**.

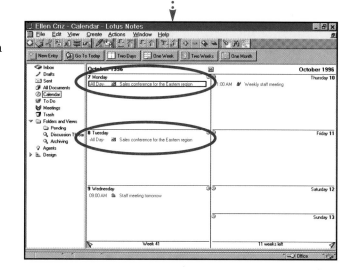

TASK **30**

Noting an Anniversary

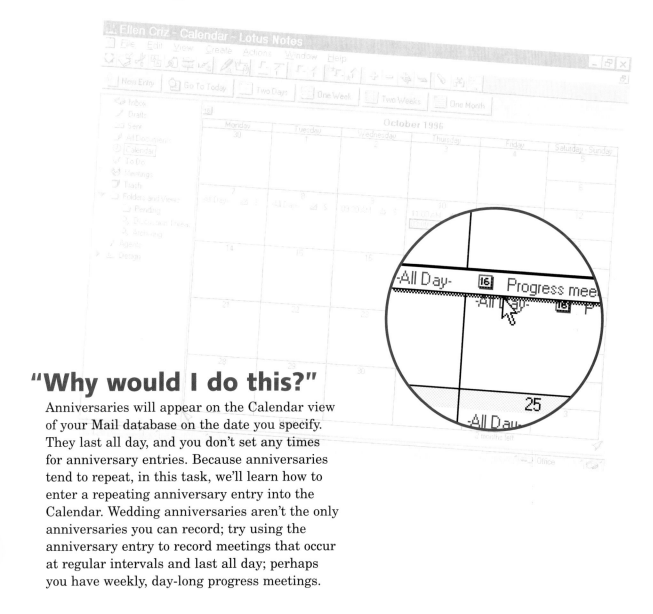

"Why would I do this?"

Anniversaries will appear on the Calendar view of your Mail database on the date you specify. They last all day, and you don't set any times for anniversary entries. Because anniversaries tend to repeat, in this task, we'll learn how to enter a repeating anniversary entry into the Calendar. Wedding anniversaries aren't the only anniversaries you can record; try using the anniversary entry to record meetings that occur at regular intervals and last all day; perhaps you have weekly, day-long progress meetings.

Task 30: Noting an Anniversary

1 In the Calendar view, select the date on which you want the anniversary to appear. Then, click the **New Entry** button on the Action bar.

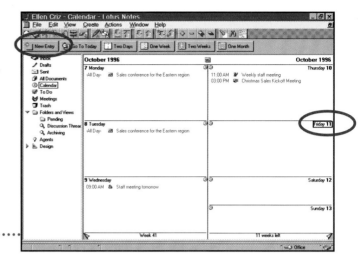

> **Puzzled?**
>
> Instead of clicking the New Entry button, you can double-click the Calendar date.

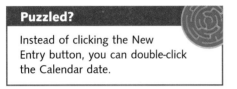

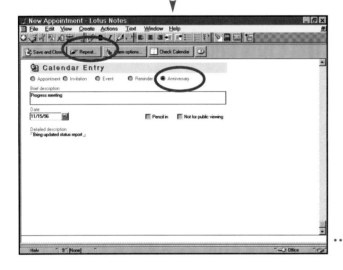

2 On the Calendar Entry document, click the **Anniversary** option button. Fill in a brief description using less than 100 characters. Use the Detailed Description text box to add information. Click the **Repeat** button to place the entry on your Calendar at regular repeating intervals.

> **Missing Link**
>
> Use the **Pencil in** checkbox for appointments that aren't certain; Notes will ignore these entries while checking for conflicts. Use the **Not for Public Viewing** checkbox to hide the appointment when others are checking your Calendar for free time.

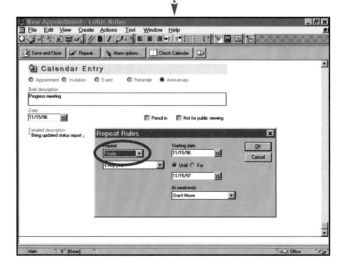

3 By default, Notes assumes that anniversaries occur annually.

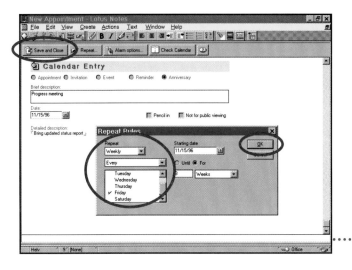

4 From the **Repeat** list boxes, select the frequency with which you want the anniversary to repeat. You can change the starting date, and you can specify an ending date using either the **Until** option button (and choose a date) or the **For** button (and specify the number of times you want the event to appear on your Calendar). Choose **OK** to save the repeating rules, and click **Save and Close** to save the anniversary entry.

Puzzled?

The choices available in the second **Repeat** list box and on the right side of the dialog box change based on what you select in the first **Repeat** list box.

5 If you switch to a Calendar view that encompasses the time frame you set up for the repeating anniversary, you'll see the entry on the Calendar at the interval you specified. ■

Missing Link

To edit an anniversary, double-click it to open it. Then, click the **Edit Document** button on the Action bar. Make your changes and choose **Save and Close**.

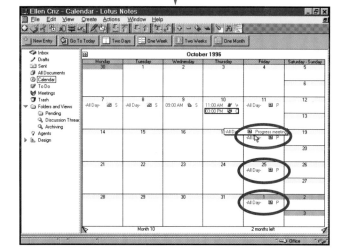

TASK 31

Inviting People to a Meeting

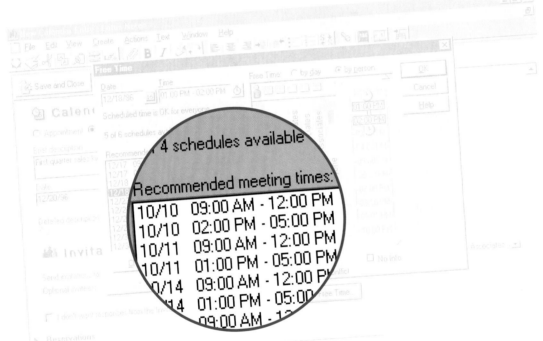

"Why would I do this?"

Invitations to meetings are similar to appointments in that you set both a date and a time. Invitations are different from appointments in that you have much more control over the scheduling of the meeting, assuming that each person you are inviting to the meeting has set their Delegation Profile so that others can view their Calendar. If so, you can view the Calendars of the other people you are inviting to the meeting, then you also can let Notes check the Calendars of all the people you intend to invite to the meeting and look for a common free time.

On each meeting invitation you create, you set the date and time of the meeting and provide a brief description and, if you want, a detailed description. You specify who you want to invite to the meeting as well as optional invitees. When Notes checks the meeting time for conflicts, Notes ignores the schedules of optional invitees. By default, Notes requests responses to your meeting invitation from the invitees (the equivalent of an R.S.V.P.), but you can indicate that you don't want responses.

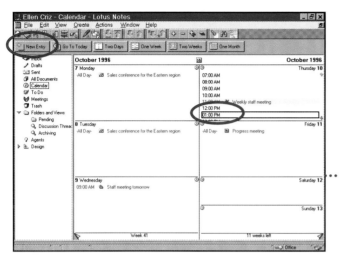

1 On the Calendar, select the date on which you want to schedule the meeting. To save time, you can click the clock to display times and click the time at which you want to schedule the meeting. Then, click the **New Entry** button on the Action bar.

Puzzled?

Instead of clicking the New Entry button, you can double-click the appointment time. Alternatively, you don't need to display appointment times; Notes will let you set the time on the Calendar Entry window.

2 On the Calendar Entry document, click the **Invitation** option button. Fill in a brief description using less than 100 characters. If necessary, change the meeting date and time. Use the Detailed Description text box to add information. Click the **Send Invitations To** list box button to invite people to your meeting.

Missing Link

Use the **Pencil in** checkbox for appointments that aren't certain; Use the **Not for Public Viewing** checkbox to hide the appointment when others check your Calendar for free time.

3 Notes displays the Names dialog box. Choose each person you want to invite to the meeting and click the **Add** button. When you finish, choose **OK** to redisplay the Calendar Entry document.

Missing Link

To add optional invitees, repeat Step 3, but start by clicking the **Optional Invitees** list box button. The Names dialog box reappears so that you can make selections.

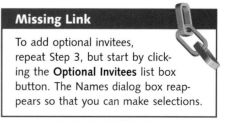

4 Make sure all your invitees are available for the meeting by clicking the **Find Free Time** button.

> ### Missing Link
>
> In the graphic representation, each vertical block represents the schedule of an invitee. Busy times are cyan, and free times are white. Unavailable schedules appear in gray.

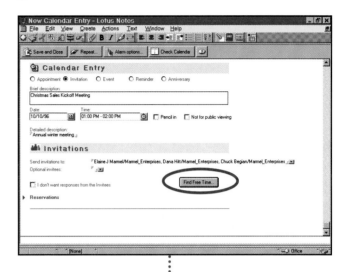

5 On the left side of the Free Time dialog box, you see that the selected time is *not* OK for everyone and that only two of the four people invited have made their schedules available. Notes suggests a series of free times from the two available schedules. On the right, you see a graphic representation of the schedules. The right-most block is a consolidation of Everyone's busy (cyan) and free times (white). The proposed meeting time appears in red in the cyan portion of that block, indicating a schedule conflict. Choose a new meeting time from the **Recommended Meeting Times**.

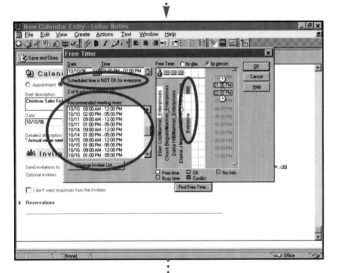

6 When you select one of the times Notes suggests, the proposed meeting time block changes to green and moves into the free (white) area. Choose **OK** to save your change. Then click **Save and Close** to save the meeting invitation. Notes will prompt you to send the meeting invitation to the invitees. ■

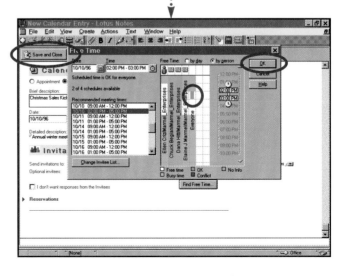

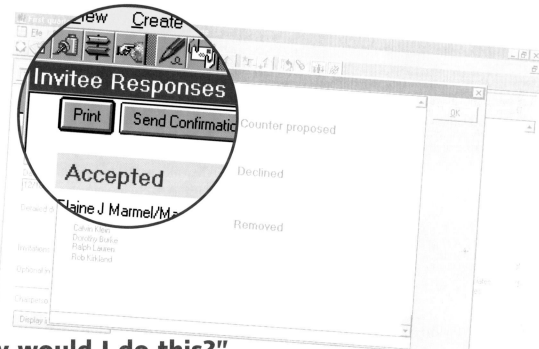

Checking the Responses to an Invitation

"Why would I do this?"

If you invite people to a meeting and you let Notes request responses to your invitation, you can also let Notes track the responses for you.

As you would expect, responses arrive as e-mail messages. However, Notes also ties the response to the original invitation, and you can view responses in two ways in your Mail database: in the Calendar view or in the Meeting view, where you see all meetings. Suppose, for example, that the meeting is approaching and you

want to see who was invited and who has responded. You can open the meeting from your Calendar and display a status report on the invitations. Alternatively, if you want to simply see who has responded, you can use the Meeting view, where Notes displays all your meetings, organized by meeting date and time (from earliest to latest), along with a list of responses to each meeting invitation.

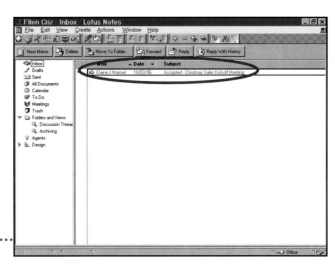

1 Initially, responses to meeting invitations appear as e-mail messages in the Inbox of your Mail database.

2 When you open the e-mail message, it will look similar to the one you see in the figure here. Click **Close** to redisplay your Inbox.

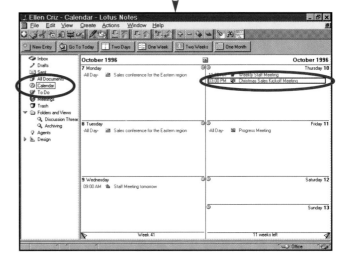

3 Click the **Calendar** view in the Navigation panel and display the date on which the meeting appears.

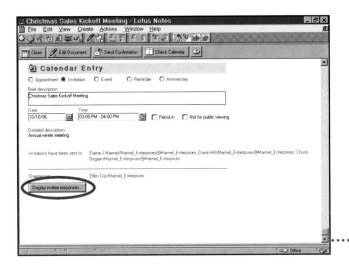

4 Double-click the meeting to open the entry. Then click the **Display Invitee Responses** button.

5 If you want to print the response list, click the **Print** button. If you click the **Send Confirmation** button, Notes sends another e-mail message to the invitees confirming the meeting will be held. Choose **OK** to return to the Calendar Entry window. Then choose **Close** to redisplay the Mail database.

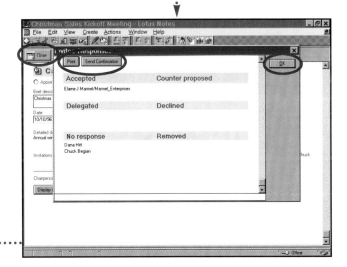

6 Click the **Meetings** view in the Navigation pane. Notes displays a list of all your scheduled meetings. The responses to meeting invitations appear immediately below the original meeting invitation. ■

Missing Link

You can re-sort meetings so that they appear from latest to earliest by clicking the carat that appears next to the Meeting Time column heading.

Responding to a Meeting Invitation

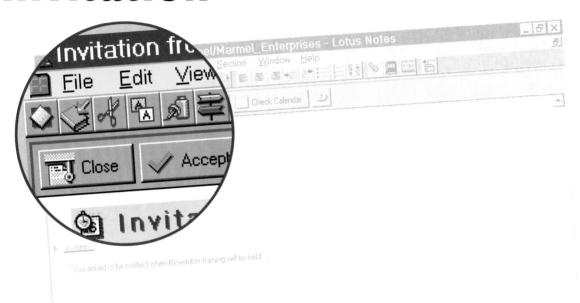

"Why would I do this?"

When you receive an invitation to a meeting, it comes in the form of an e-mail message. But when you open the message, you'll see some special buttons available to help you appropriately process the message. For example, you may need to check your Calendar to determine if you can attend the meeting. If you can't, you may need to find a date you can propose as an alternative, or you may want to propose that someone else attend the meeting instead of you.

If you decide to delegate the meeting, Notes won't let you also propose alternative dates or times—which makes perfect sense. If you're not going to be there, you shouldn't care when or where the meeting is held.

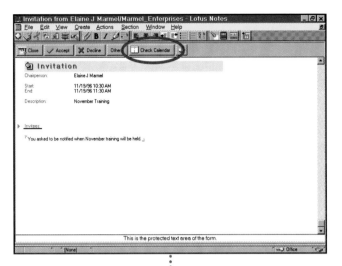

1 Double-click the message to open it and respond to it. Click the **Check Calendar** button on the Action bar to view your Calendar to see if you're available for the meeting.

Missing Link

If you plan to propose an alternative date, you might want to create a Calendar entry and choose the **Pencil In** checkbox.

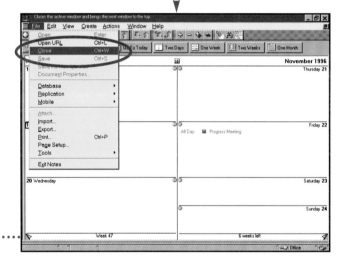

2 Notes opens the Calendar to the proposed meeting date. If you're not available on that date, you can navigate through this Calendar view as described in Task 26 to find an alternative date. When you finish viewing your Calendar, open the **File** menu and choose **Close** to redisplay the invitation.

3 At this point, you can accept or decline the invitation (click **Accept** or **Decline** on the Action bar) or you can propose alternatives to the initiator of the meeting. To propose an alternative date or send someone to the meeting on your behalf, click the **Other** button on the Action bar.

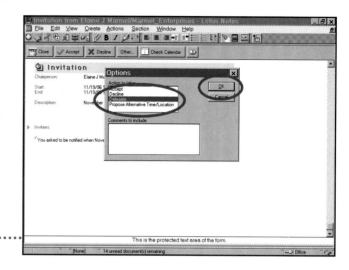

4 Notes displays the Options dialog box. To send someone else to the meeting, choose **Delegate** and then choose **OK**.

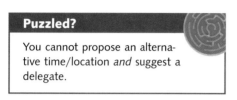

> **Puzzled?**
>
> You cannot propose an alternative time/location *and* suggest a delegate.

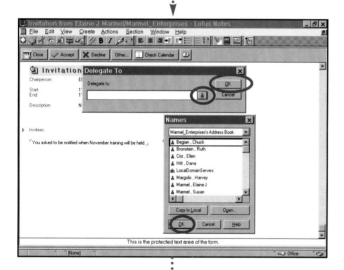

5 Notes displays the Delegate To dialog box. Click the button at the right edge of the text box to display your address book, from which you can choose a delegate. Choose **OK** to return to the Delegate To dialog box. Choose **OK** to return to the Invitation. Notes displays a dialog box, informing you that an invitation has been sent to the delegate and a notice has been sent to the initiator of the meeting saying you won't be attending. When you choose **OK**, Notes redisplays the Inbox of the Mail database.

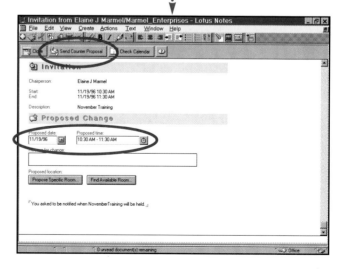

6 Alternatively, if you plan to attend but want to propose a change, you can choose **Propose Alternative Time/Location** in the Options dialog box in Step 4 and then click **OK**. Notes changes the Invitation document so that you can propose an alternative date, time, or location, and provide a reason for the alternatives you propose. When you finish, click the **Send Counter Proposal** button on the Action bar. ■

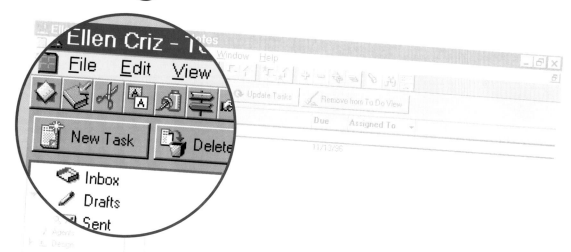

Creating a To Do List Task

"Why would I do this?"

I couldn't survive without my To Do list, that lifeline on which I place and prioritize tasks I need to accomplish. The tasks that might appear on a To Do list are not necessarily date-dependent; sometimes, you just need to make a list of things you need to do and then order them by their importance. In addition to the Calendar, Notes provides the To Do view in your Mail database, where you can set up and manage a To Do list. The Task document you complete to place an item in the To Do view is very flexible; the only field you *must* complete to be allowed to save the task is the Subject.

While the tasks on a To Do list are not necessarily date-dependent, getting things done is often determined by whether you have time today to

accomplish a particular task. And, sometimes, you want to schedule a task for a specific date—if only to assure yourself that you get the task done by a deadline. Notes' To Do feature is particularly useful because you can optionally choose to display a task in both the To Do view and the Calendar view by assigning a Start Date to the task.

To make sure things don't slip through the cracks, place the task on your To Do list even if you don't know when you're going to get to it—just leave the Start Date blank on the Task document. Later, when you determine the Start Date, edit the task, assign the Start Date, and then display the task in your Calendar.

1 Open your **Mail** database and, in the Navigation pane, click the **To Do** view. Click the **New Task** button on the Action bar.

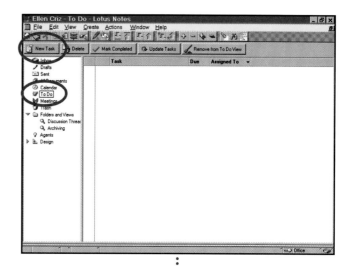

> **Missing Link**
>
> You can convert a mail message to a task. Open the message and then choose **Actions**, **Convert to Task**. Notes converts the mail message to a task and gives you the opportunity to modify the task.

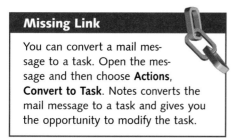

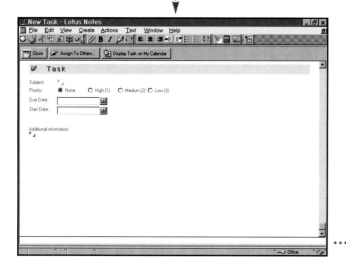

2 Notes displays the Task document.

3 In the **Subject** text box, type the description you want to appear when you view the task from the To Do view. Choose a **Priority** option button for the task and assign a **Due Date** and **Start** date. Use the **Additional Information** text box to further describe the task.

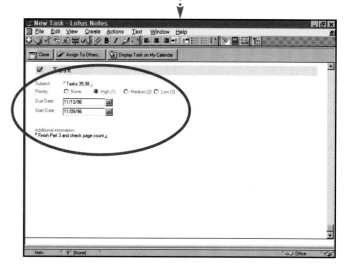

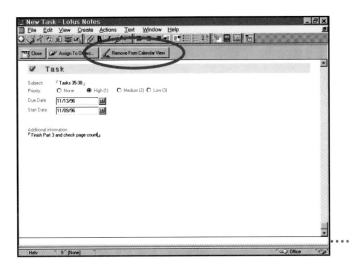

4 If you supplied a Due Date, as I did, you can optionally choose to see the task on your Calendar. Click the **Display Task on My Calendar** button on the Action bar. If you click this button, Notes changes the button to the Remove From Calendar View button so that you can hide the task from your Calendar view. The task will, however, remain in the To Do view.

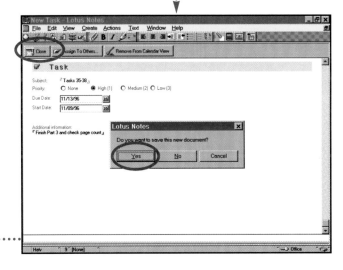

5 Click the **Close** button on the Action bar. Notes asks if you want to save the task; click **Yes**.

6 To see your task in the Calendar, click the **Calendar** view in the Navigation pane. Then, display the Start Date you assigned to the Task. ■

Missing Link

Need to assign a Start Date to a task you previously created? To edit the task, highlight it and double-click. Assign a start date, and then choose **Display in Task on My Calendar** from the Action bar.

Assigning a Task to Others

"Why would I do this?"

OK, here's my favorite part. One surefire way to get a task off your desk is to give it to someone else to do. If you're in the fortunate position of being able to assign tasks to other people, Notes helps you set up the task and then delegate responsibility to someone else. When you assign a task to someone else, Notes sends that person an e-mail, informing him of the task. Be aware that assigning a task to someone else is no guarantee the task will be done; the delegate can reject the task, just as you can reject a task someone tries to assign to you. When you receive an e-mail notice that someone has

assigned a task to you, you'll also notice a **Please Reassign** button on the Action bar. If you click that button, Notes sends a return e-mail to the initiator that essentially rejects the assignment of the task. (Is everybody breathing a sigh of relief now?)

You can delegate a task as you create it or later (perhaps when you realize you don't have time to do it). In this task, we'll edit an existing task and assign it to someone else.

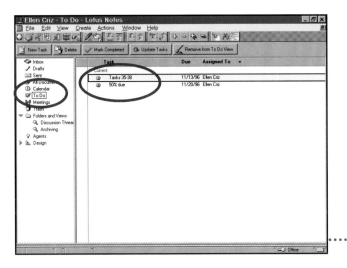

1 In the To Do view, highlight the task you want to delegate and double-click to open it.

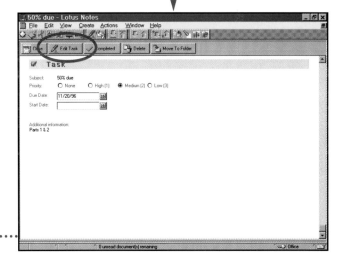

2 Click **Edit Task** in the Action bar.

3 Click **Assign To Others** in the Action bar.

4 To assign an address from an Address Book, click **Address** in the Action bar. Select an address book and a person and click the **To** button to place his address in the list. Click **OK** to redisplay the Task document.

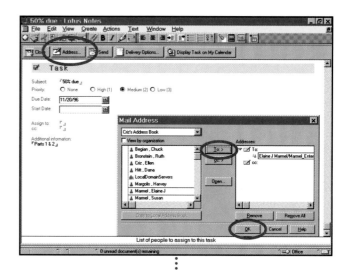

Puzzled?

If you prefer, you can, type the address of the person to whom you want to assign the task in the **Assign To** text box.

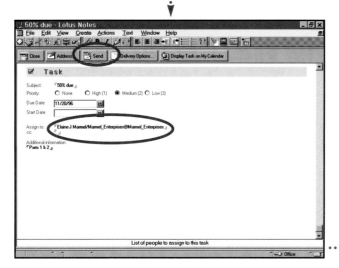

5 The name and e-mail address of the person to whom you are assigning the task appear on the Task document. Click the **Send** button on the Action bar.

6 Notes saves your changes, sends an e-mail to the person you selected, and redisplays the To Do view of your Mail database. Notice the task now assigned to the person you selected. ■

Missing Link

You can assign a task to as many people as you want; Notes will send each an e-mail and place the task in the To Do view of each person.

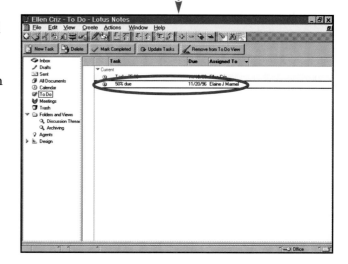

Reviewing Tasks and Cleaning House

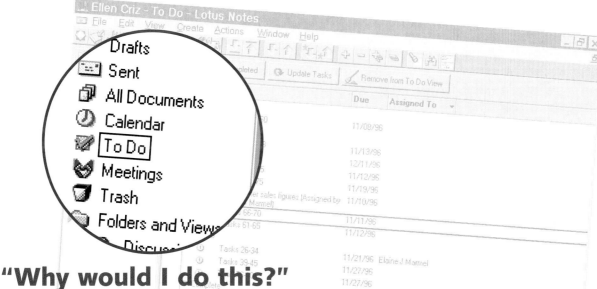

"Why would I do this?"

The To Do view displays tasks you create and messages that ask you to respond by a specified date. By default, items in the To Do view appear in one of four categories: Overdue, Current, Future, or Completed. You may also see a "Rejected" category, which shows tasks you assigned to others that they rejected as well as tasks others assigned to you that you rejected. Within each category, tasks appear in the To Do view in order of priority. Messages you receive that ask you to respond by a particular date don't have a priority. Tasks or messages without priorities appear after all the tasks in the category with a priority. All tasks with the same priority (even if that priority is "None") will appear in order of due date.

As time goes by, tasks may need to move from one category to another. To manage your To Do

view, you'll want to update the To Do view to ensure that tasks appear in the correct category. In addition, as you complete tasks, you may want to mark them completed, if only to attain a sense of accomplishment. You may also decide that you no longer need to see a task in the To Do view—either it's complete or it no longer needs to be completed. You may want to delete the task (the process is the same you learned for deleting mail), or you may want to remove a task from the To Do view. For example, you may want to remove completed tasks or messages requesting a response by a particular date. (You can't mark a message in the To Do view as completed.)

Task 36: Reviewing Tasks and Cleaning House

1 When you select the To Do view from the Navigation pane, you'll see your tasks organized into categories and sorted by priority and then due date. To update the To Do view and ensure that all tasks appear in the correct category, click the **Update Tasks** button on the Action bar.

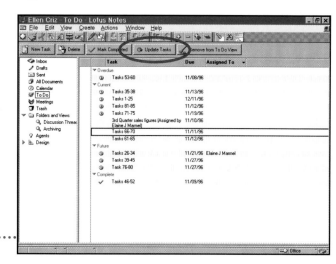

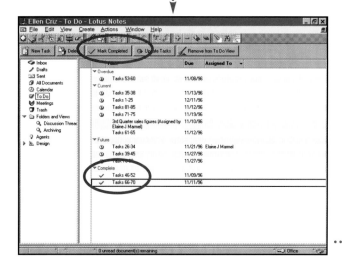

2 To complete a task, highlight it and click the **Mark Completed** button on the Action bar.

Puzzled?

If you accidentally mark a task completed, open the **To Do** view, choose **Actions**, **Unmark Completed**.

3 To remove a message from the To Do view, highlight the message and click the **Remove from To Do View** button. ■

Missing Link

Removing a message from the To Do view doesn't affect any other view in the Mail database. But deleting a message or a task works the same as deleting mail—first Notes marks the item for deletion by placing a Trash can in the leftmost column of the view. When you refresh the view or exit Notes, then Notes permanently deletes the item.

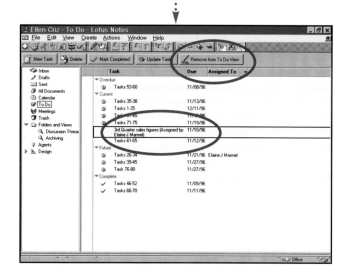

PART IV

Using Notes Databases and Documents

REMEMBER, NOTES USES the term database to compartmentalize information that you might want to share in a single area of interest. Notes databases, therefore, are not necessarily like traditional databases. For example, when you use mail in Notes, you are using the Mail database. And (as you saw in Part II), you might also use the Address Book database in conjunction with the Mail database when you send mail.

Some of the databases you use are created automatically when Notes is installed, but most are created by someone in your company. Throughout this part, I'll use, as an example database, a Training database that I built. The Training database is similar to one that computer trainers might create (now why doesn't that surprise you?) and contains information about training classes people can attend. If you don't find a similar database on your system, don't worry; you can perform the tasks described in this part on almost any database you find on your system.

Notes databases reside on a server so that everyone using Notes can access the database. Initially, you'll learn to create an icon that helps you easily open and close the database on the server. After that, you'll learn how to create a copy of the database that you can use on your own computer instead of on the server. When you use the copy, you can make changes to the database while you are not connected to the server.

Regardless of the database in which you are working, certain commands work consistently. For example, you can open, close, copy, remove, and add all databases on your Workspace in the same way. You also use the same technique to open and close documents in each database. This consistency across databases makes it easy to use and share any database on the system.

You can also search for and preview documents instead of reading every document in the database.

Some of the things you'll learn to do with Notes databases in this section include:

- You can add documents to databases (only if your privileges in that database allow it). Also, you can edit documents using various features (like moving and copying text, and changing the formatting of the text).

- Use Document links (known as DocLinks in Notes), which provide a way for you to switch a reader from the current document to another document, view, folder, or even database.

- Use Text Hotspots, which are highlighted text that pop up and provide additional information or perform an action when you click them; in this part, you'll learn how to create and use a pop-up hotspot.

- You can import data from spreadsheets or text files into Notes. When you import data, you actually bring information from an outside file into a Notes database.

Just as different databases have different buttons available in the Action bar, different databases also contain different views. For example, you can organize your Address Book database so that documents (names and addresses) for companies appear in the Companies view, while documents for individuals appear in the People view. You can switch views by simply clicking on the view you want to see in the Navigation pane.

You also can create categories in a database, assign documents to a category, and then view the documents by category. And, anyone who can view the database and edit the documents can create categories and assign documents to the categories.

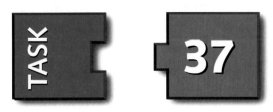

TASK **37**

Searching for Databases on the Server

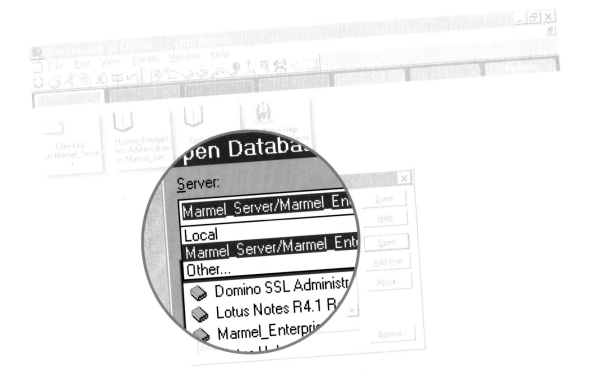

"Why would I do this?"

Notes uses the term *database* to refer to compartmentalized information that you might want to share. Since you're sharing the information, Notes databases are stored on the server. In this task, you'll learn how to locate the databases on a server and find a description for each database.

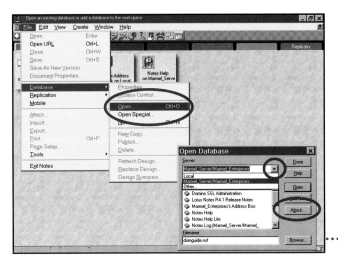

1 Open the **File** menu and choose the **Database** command. From the submenu, choose **Open**. The Open Database dialog box appears. Open the **Server** list box to identify available Servers and click one. Notes displays the databases available on the selected server. Highlight a database in the Database list and choose **About**.

2 Notes displays the About This Database page for the highlighted database. When you finish reading the database description, choose **Close**.

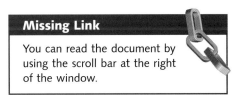

Missing Link

You can read the document by using the scroll bar at the right of the window.

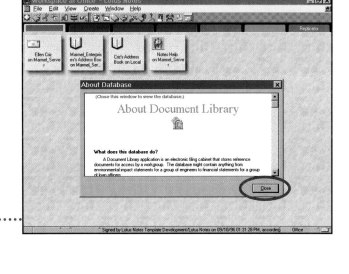

3 Notes redisplays the Open Database dialog box. Choose **Done** to close the dialog box. ∎

TASK

38

Adding a Database to Your Workspace

"Why would I do this?"

Suppose, after browsing through the databases on the server, you find a database that interests you. And, you know you're going to want to use that database regularly. You can add an icon for the database to your Notes Workspace so that you can easily open the database on the server.

Adding databases can be a little tricky because you need to know the server on which they are

stored before you can add them to your Workspace. Don't worry; you will soon become familiar enough with your Notes network to easily navigate it and find the databases you need. And, in the meantime, your network administrator can help you by identifying servers that contain Notes databases which you can access.

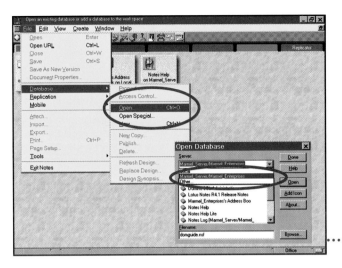

1 Open the **File** menu and choose the **Database** command. From the submenu, choose **Open**. The Open Database dialog box appears. Open the **Server** list box to identify available Servers and click one.

2 Highlight the database you want to add to your Workspace and click the **Open** button.

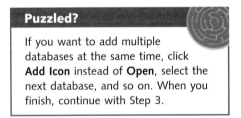

Puzzled?

If you want to add multiple databases at the same time, click **Add Icon** instead of **Open**, select the next database, and so on. When you finish, continue with Step 3.

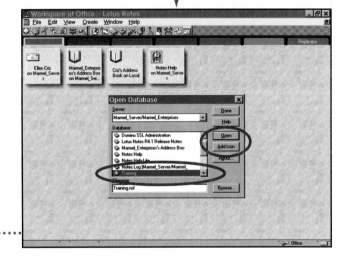

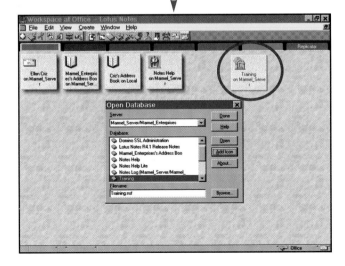

3 The icon for the database appears on your Workspace. Click **Done** to close the Open Database dialog box. ▪

Copying a Database to Your Local Machine

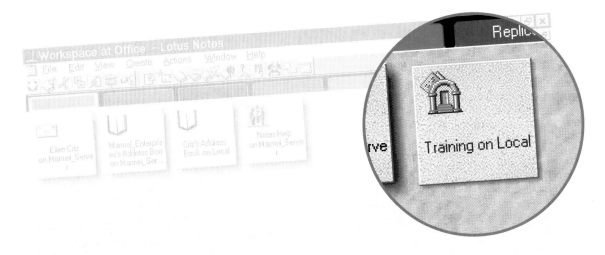

"Why would I do this?"

Under some circumstances, you may want to copy a database to your local machine. Suppose your company stores standard forms that everybody in the company uses. You could copy this database to your machine because you don't intend to make changes to these documents.

Making a local copy of a database is particularly useful if you want to be able to use a database

even if the Notes server is down. But be aware that you don't want to use this type of database copy if you plan to make changes to the database and then upload those changes. You need a local *replica* for that kind of activity, not a local *copy*. You'll learn how to make a local replica later in the book.

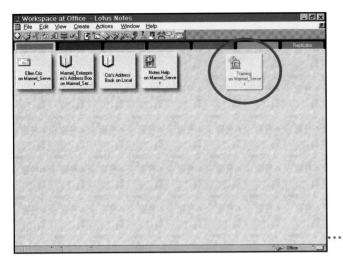

1 If you haven't already added an icon for the database you want to copy to your Workspace, do so following the steps in the last task. Click the icon for the database to select the database on your Workspace.

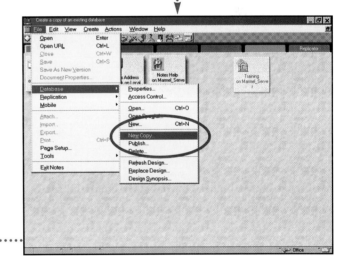

2 Open the **File** menu and choose **Database**. From the submenu, choose **New Copy**.

3 Make sure Local appears in the Server list box. If you want to change the title of the database, change it in the Title text box.

115

4 Remove the check from the Access Control List to ensure you have access to the database after you copy it.

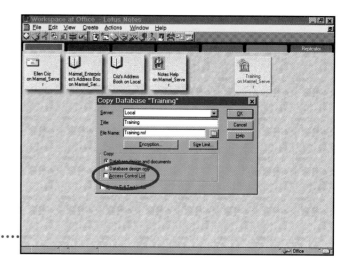

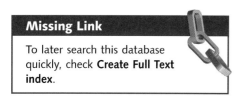

Missing Link

To later search this database quickly, check **Create Full Text index**.

5 Choose **OK**. Notes copies the database to your computer. A new icon appears on your Workspace tab containing the database name and the words on `Local`. ■

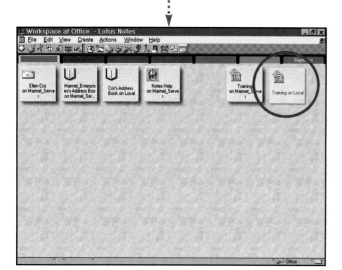

Missing Link

You can work in this local database even if the server is not operating. However, if you make changes to this database copy, you *cannot* update the database on the server. To update a server database with changes made locally, you must make a different kind of copy—a local *replica*, which you'll learn about later in the book.

Searching for Documents

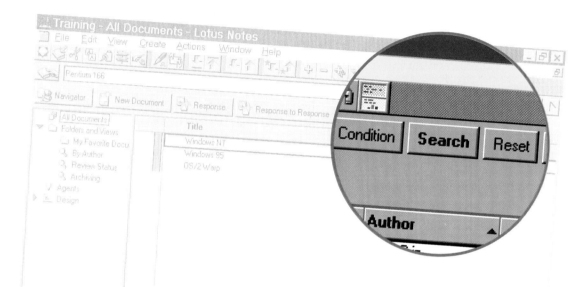

"Why would I do this?"

To help you quickly find documents that might
be of interest to you, you can search for them.
The designer of the database usually builds a
list of words (called the full text index) that are
found in documents in the database. When the
database contains a full text index, you can
create a more complex search using the Search
Builder dialog box; from this dialog box, you can
search for any or all of eight different words or
phrases, or you can set other search criteria
such as searching for documents by Author or
by date. You'll know that the database contains
a full text index if you see the Add Condition
button on the Search Bar; you'll learn to use the
Search Bar in this task.

You also can search multiple databases simultaneously if you select them before you start the
following steps. Hold down the **Shift** key and
click each database on your Workspace that you
want to search. While still holding the **Shift**
key, open any one of the selected databases.
Notes displays all the views for the first selected
database; all other selected databases appear at
the bottom of the Navigation pane. After you
perform a search using the following steps,
Notes displays the result for the first selected
database; to see the results for other databases,
select a view for one from the Navigation pane.

1 Open the database you want to search.

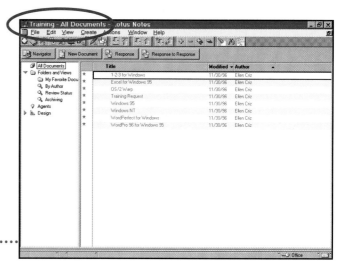

Puzzled?

If this is the first time you have opened this database, you may see the About This Database document. Press **Esc** or choose **File, Close** to close the document. All document titles will appear in pink with red stars next to them, indicating you have not yet read them.

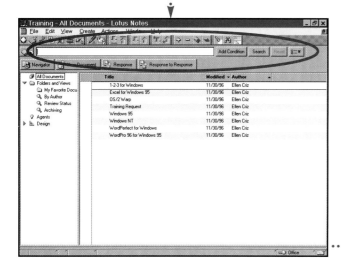

2 Open the **View** menu and choose **Search Bar** to display the Search Bar above the action bar.

Missing Link

To make things easier to read in the figure, we marked all documents as read by choosing **Edit, Unread Marks, Mark All Read**.

3 Click in the text box in the Search Bar and type the characters for which you want to search. Click the **Search** button, and Notes displays the documents found that match what you typed.

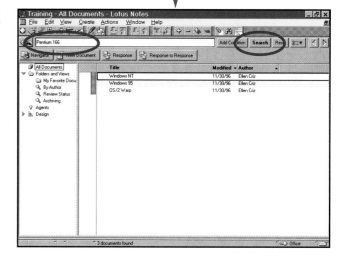

Missing Link

The more characters you type, the fewer matches Notes is likely to find because Notes tries to match exactly what you typed. The more characters you type, the more you limit the search.

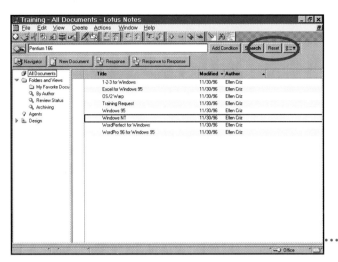

4 To redisplay all documents, click the **Reset** button in the Search Bar.

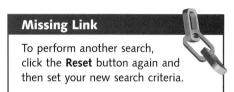

Missing Link

To perform another search, click the **Reset** button again and then set your new search criteria.

5 If the database is fully indexed, you can click the **Add Condition** button to display the Search Builder and create a more complex search.

Puzzled?

If you are a manager or designer of a database or if you have created a replica, you'll see a Create Index button if the database does not contain a full text index. Be careful about choosing this button; if the database is large, the action could take a very long time, and then you'll need to update the index you create periodically.

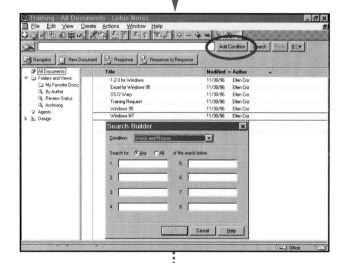

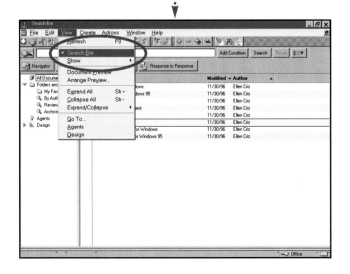

6 To close the Search Bar, reopen the **View** menu and choose **Search Bar** again to remove the check you see next to the Search Bar command. ■

Previewing a Document

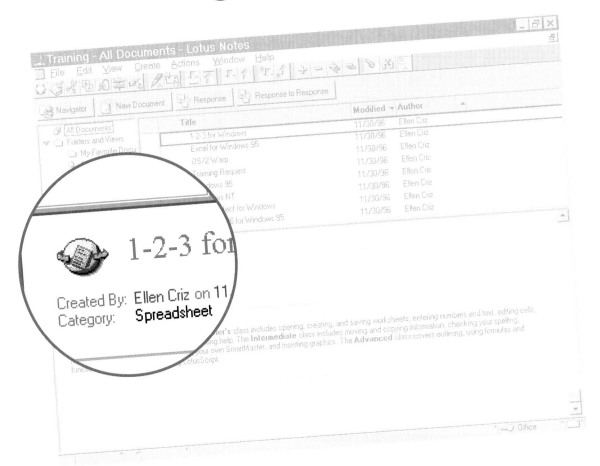

"Why would I do this?"

You can view the contents of a document without opening it by previewing it. When you preview, you display a third pane in the Notes window, in addition to the Navigation pane on the left and the View pane on the right. In the Preview pane, you can read a selected document without opening it.

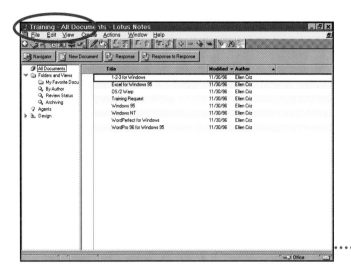

1 Open a database and highlight a document you want to preview.

2 Open the **View** menu and choose **Document Preview**.

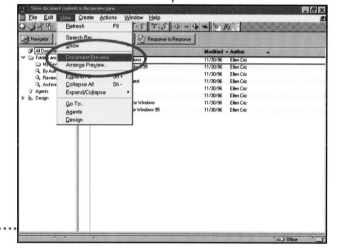

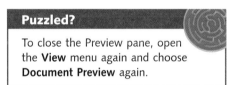

Puzzled?

To close the Preview pane, open the **View** menu again and choose **Document Preview** again.

3 Notes opens a Preview pane at the bottom of the screen and displays the contents of the highlighted document. If you can't see all of the document, use the scroll bar at the right edge of the screen. ▓

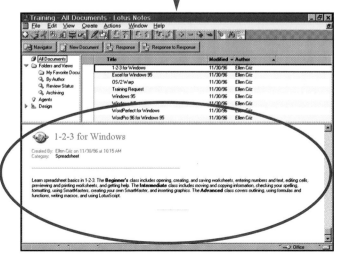

Missing Link

To preview a different document, click that document to select it. Notes changes the contents of the Preview pane. Note that previewing a document in the Preview pane *does not* mark the document as "read."

121

TASK 42

Creating and Saving a New Document

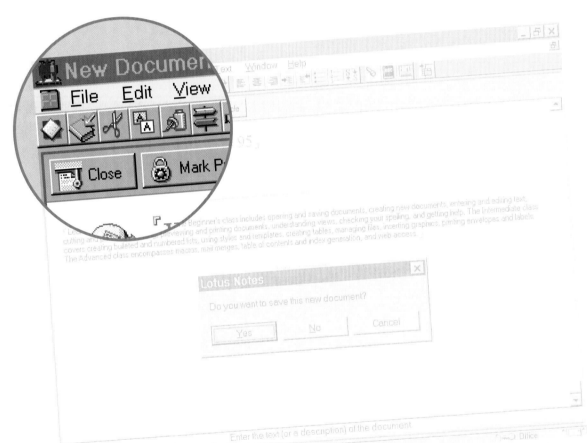

"Why would I do this?"

If you have the correct rights to a database, you can add documents to that database. You'll use a predefined form in the database to create the document. The form is part of the database's template, and it may not be called "New Document"; in fact, you may see a button titled "Create." The form will contain, at a minimum,

one set of brackets that represent a subject field—you'll place the document title in these brackets. The document title appears in at least one view in the database. The form may also contain other fields that will appear as brackets or possibly as list boxes or option buttons.

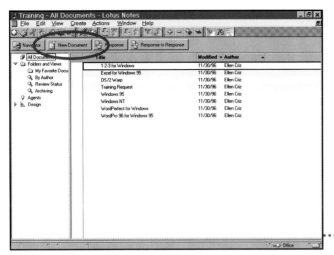

1 Click the **New Document** button in the Action bar. If you don't see a New Document button in your database, open the **Create** menu and choose the appropriate form to create; all forms you can create appear on the Create menu.

2 Notes displays a new, blank document ready for you to complete. At the top of the document, fill in a title for the document as you want it to appear in the View pane; for example, Word 8 for Windows 95. Finish the rest of the form as appropriate. Click the **Close** button in the Action bar or press **Esc** and choose **Yes** in the dialog box to save the document.

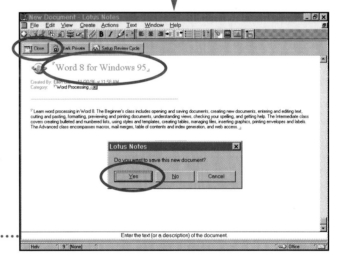

3 Notes redisplays the database, and your document appears in the View pane. ■

Missing Link

Most of the rest of the tasks in this part teach you techniques to use while creating or editing documents.

Moving and Copying Text

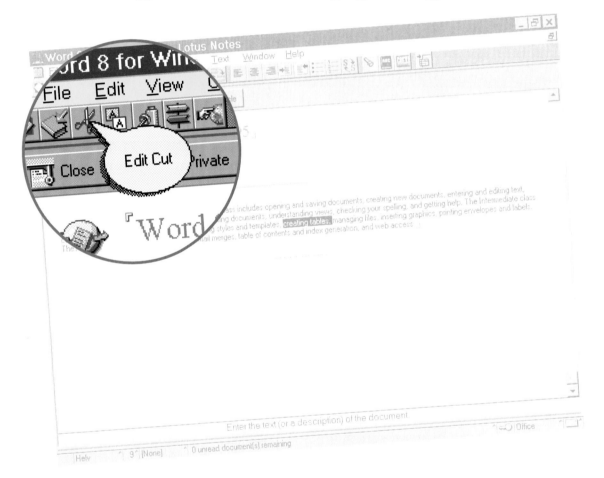

"Why would I do this?"

Suppose you type some text and later decide it would make more sense in another location. You can move the text. Or suppose you type some text that also needs to appear at another location. You can copy the text to another area in your document or in another document.

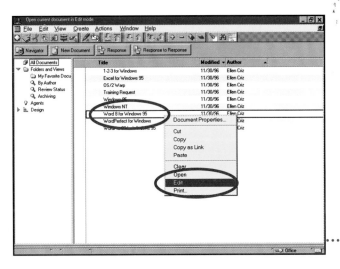

1 To open a document and edit it, point at the document, press the right mouse button, and choose **Edit** from the shortcut menu. Reopen the document we created in the last task.

2 Select the text you want to move or copy by dragging over the text. To move the text, click the **Cut** SmartIcon. Or open the **Edit** menu and choose the **Cut** command. Notes removes the highlighted text.

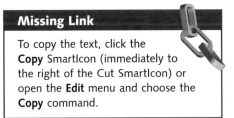

Missing Link

To copy the text, click the **Copy** SmartIcon (immediately to the right of the Cut SmartIcon) or open the **Edit** menu and choose the **Copy** command.

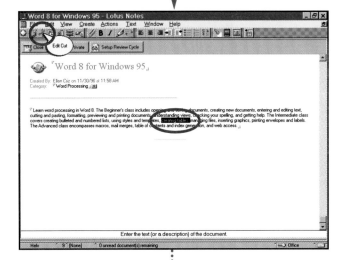

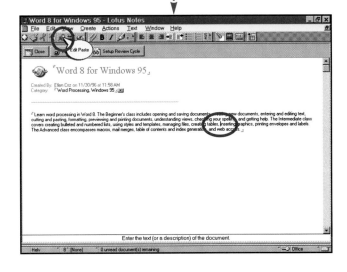

3 Place the insertion point immediately after where you want the text to appear and click the **Paste** SmartIcon. Notes displays the text at the new location in front of the insertion point. ■

Undoing Changes

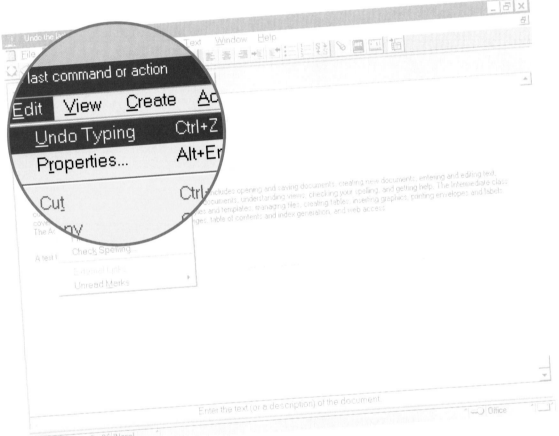

"Why would I do this?"

If you realize immediately that you've made a mistake, you can use Notes' Undo feature to correct the action. When you undo your last action, Notes restores conditions to the way they were immediately before you took your last action. Remember, though, that Undo only corrects your last action, and you can't undo all actions. For example, you cannot undo opening a database or a document. Instead, you must close the database or document.

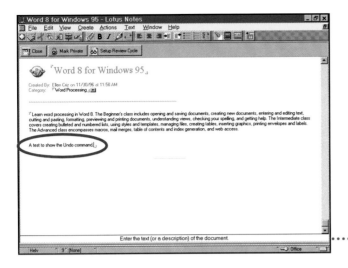

1 Open a document in edit mode and type some text.

Missing Link

To open a document to edit it, highlight it in the View pane, right-click the mouse, and choose **Edit**.

2 Open the **Edit** menu and choose the **Undo Typing** command.

Missing Link

You may not always see "undo Typing" because the word after "undo" changes, depending on the action you are undoing.

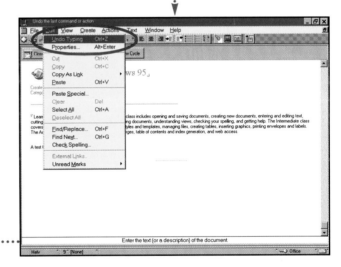

3 Notes removes the typing from your screen. ■

TASK

45

Enhancing Text

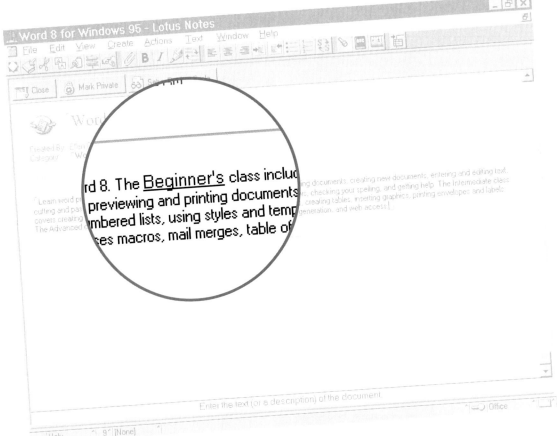

"Why would I do this?"

You can apply text attributes such as boldface, italics, or underline to various portions of your document to enhance the document. Be aware that only some kinds of fields—rich text fields—can be formatted with text attributes. You'll know if you're in a rich text field if you check the left side of the status bar at the bottom of the window and you see a font.

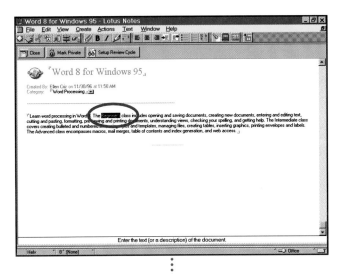

1 In a document opened in edit mode or in a new document you are creating, select the text you want to enhance.

Puzzled?

When you apply Bold, Italic, or Underline, you'll see a check mark next to them on the menu. To remove one of these enhancements, reopen the menu and choose the enhancement again. To remove all of them, reopen the **Text** menu and choose **Normal Text**.

2 Open the **Text** menu and choose the enhancement you want to make, such as underlining. You can choose from the choices listed in the third section of the menu.

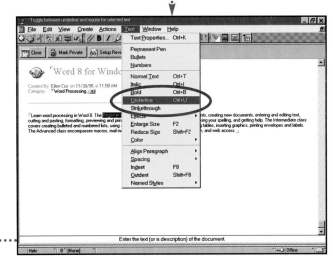

Missing Link

If you're applying boldface or italics, you can click the **Text Bold** or **Text Italic** SmartIcons.

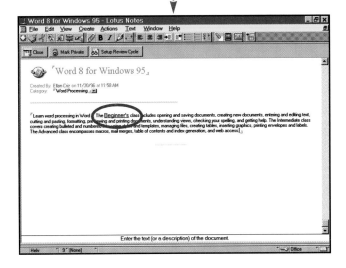

3 To enlarge the selected text, press **F2** or reopen the **Text** menu and choose **Enlarge Size**. Notes makes the selected text bigger. ■

Missing Link

When you press Shift+F2 or choose **Reduce Size** from the **Text** menu, Notes reduces the size of selected text in the same increments it increases size.

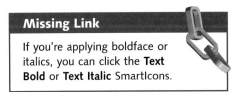

46

Listing Items Using Bullets or Numbers

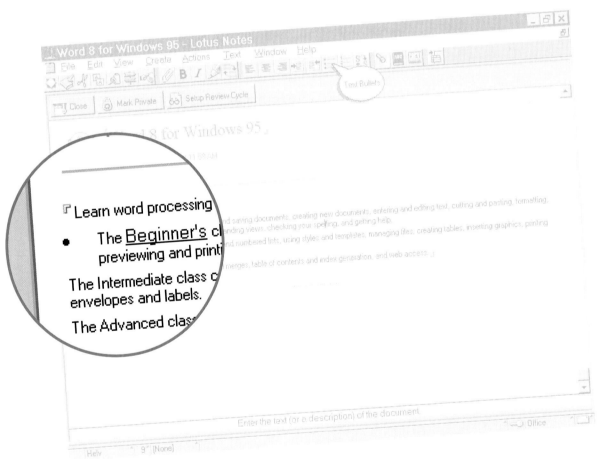

"Why would I do this?"

Upon occasion, you may want to list items in a document using either bullets or numbers to separate the items in the list. Notes will insert a bullet for you or automatically insert the next number in the list.

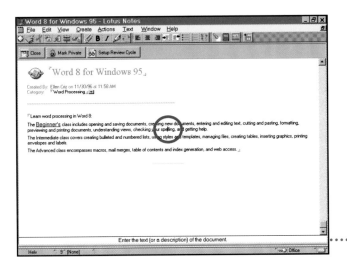

1 In a new document or in a document opened in edit mode, place the insertion point in the paragraph to which you want to add a bullet or number. Or, if necessary, press **Enter** to create a paragraph where you want a bullet to appear.

2 To add a bullet before the paragraph, click the **Text Bullets** SmartIcon.

Puzzled?

To remove a bullet, place the insertion point anywhere in a paragraph containing a bullet and click the **Text Bullets** SmartIcon.

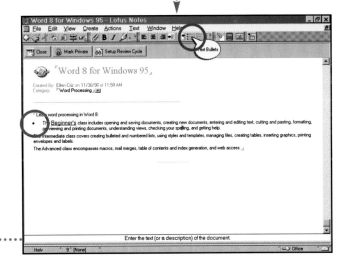

3 To add a number to the paragraph containing the insertion point, click the **Text Numbers** SmartIcon. ■

Puzzled?

You remove a number the same way you remove a bullet; place the insertion point anywhere in the paragraph containing the number and click the **Text Numbers** SmartIcon.

TASK

47

Setting Tabs

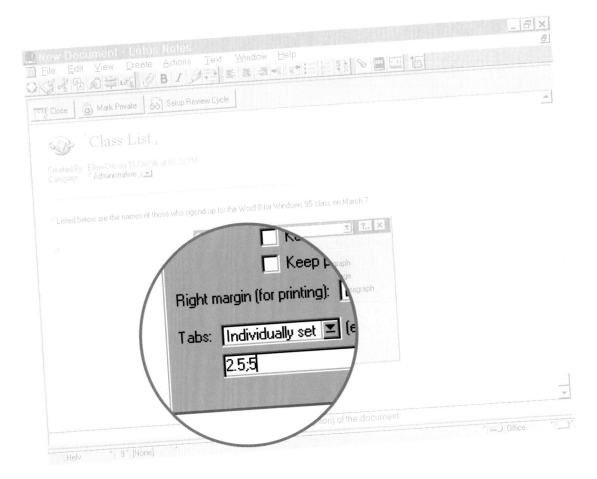

"Why would I do this?"

By default, Notes provides tabs every 1/2 inch. You might find that you can create a particular document much easier if you can establish a particular set of tabs and align material at those tabs. And, you can.

■▲●■▲●■▲●■▲●■

Task 47: Setting Tabs

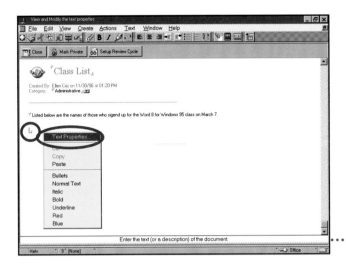

1 In a document opened in edit mode, place the insertion point at the location where you want the tab settings to take effect. Click the right mouse button to display a shortcut menu. Choose **Text Properties**.

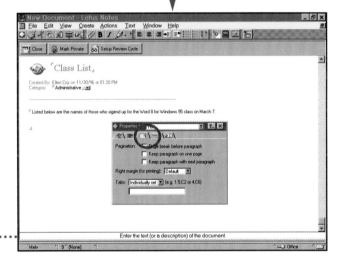

2 When the Text Properties InfoBox appears, click the third tab.

3 To set tabs that are equal distances apart, choose **Evenly spaced** from the Tabs list box. To set tabs at specific locations, choose **Individually set** from the Tabs list box.

4 In the text box below the Tab list box, type the location, in inches, where you want Notes to set tabs.

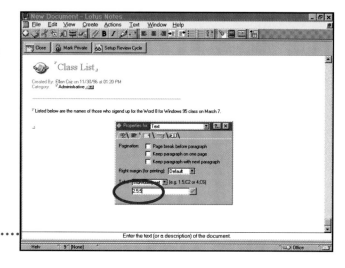

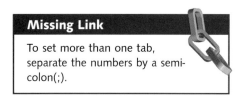

Missing Link

To set more than one tab, separate the numbers by a semi-colon(;).

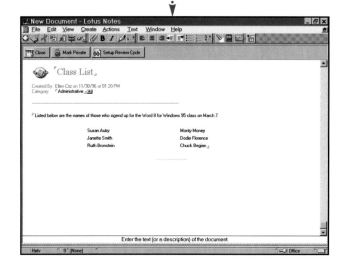

5 Close the Text Properties InfoBox (click the **X** in the upper right corner of the box), and type in your document. You'll find tabs at the locations you specified. ■

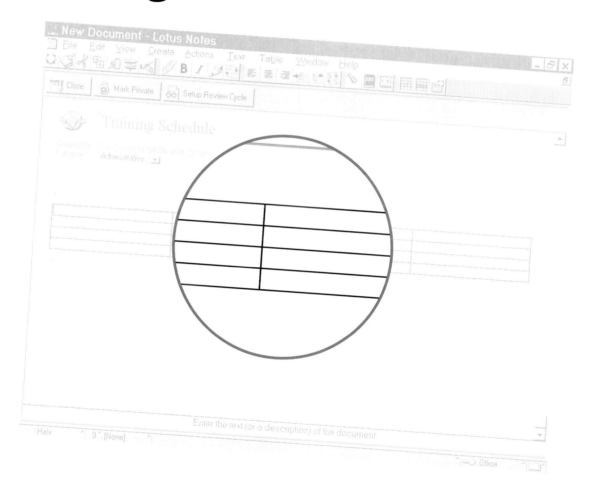

Creating Tables

"Why would I do this?"

Sometimes, tables work more efficiently than setting tabs, particularly when you need to organize your information into multiple columns. You can create tables in a Notes document.

Task 48: Creating Tables

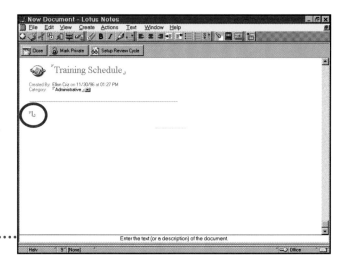

1 Open a new document or open an existing document in edit mode and place the insertion point where you want the table to appear.

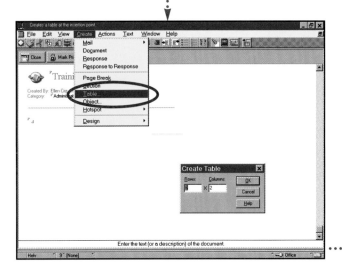

2 Open the **Create** menu and choose **Table**. Notes displays the Create Table dialog box. Type the number of rows and columns you want for your table. Choose **OK**.

3 Notes displays the table in your document. ■

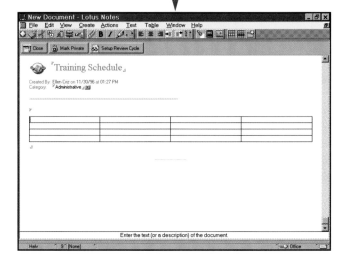

Puzzled?

Use the commands on the **Table** menu to format your table. Since the Table menu is context-sensitive, it will only appear when the insertion point is in the table.

Finding and Replacing Text

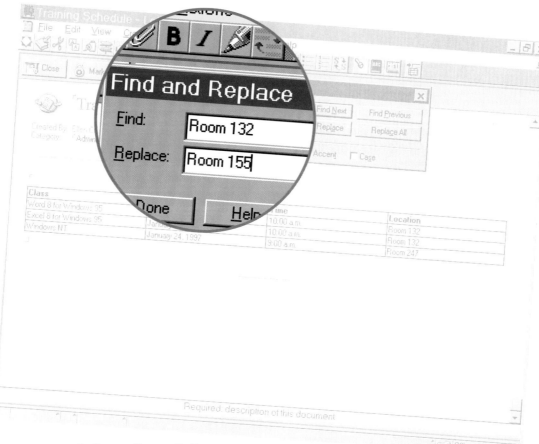

"Why would I do this?"

Suppose you create a rather lengthy document. When you finish and reread the document, you decide that you want to change a particular phrase you used throughout the document. You can use the Find and Replace feature in Notes to find text in documents and change it. As you search, you can replace single occurrences or all occurrences of text you find. If you choose to replace all occurrences, Notes warns you that you cannot undo the results of replacing all occurrences, and gives you the opportunity to cancel the operation.

1 Open an existing document in edit mode and place the insertion point at the top of the document. Then, open the **Edit** menu and choose the **Find/Replace** command.

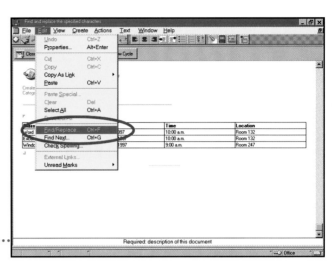

2 In the Find text box, type the word or words for which you want Notes to search.

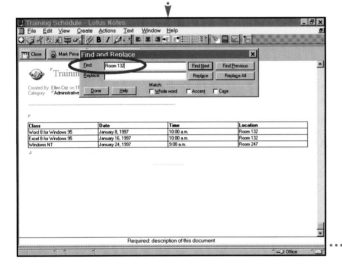

3 In the Replace text box, type the word or words you want Notes to substitute each time it finds the word for which you are searching.

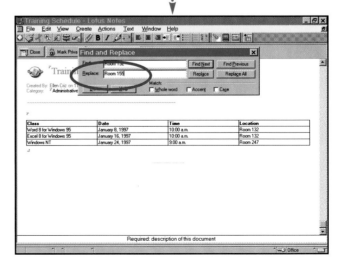

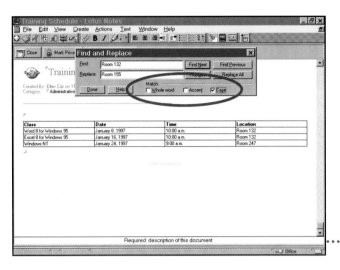

4 Use the checkboxes at the bottom of the Find and Replace dialog box to specify your search more exactly. For example, place a check in the **Case** checkbox if you want Notes to search for words that match the capitalization you used in the Find text box.

5 Choose **Find Next** to find the next occurrence of the text for which you're searching.

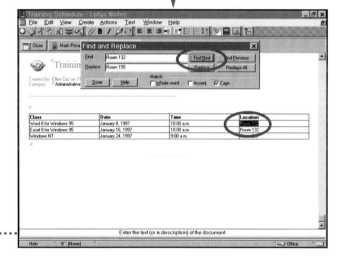

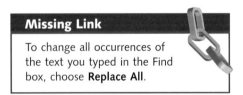

Missing Link

To change all occurrences of the text you typed in the Find box, choose **Replace All**.

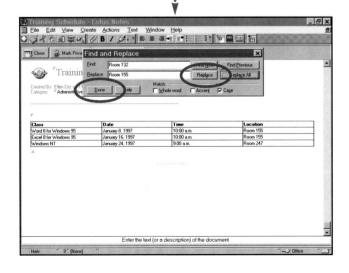

6 Choose **Replace** to replace the occurrence Notes found with the text you typed in the Replace box. When you finish searching and replacing, choose **Done** to close the Find and Replace text box. ■

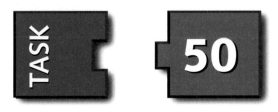

TASK 50

Checking Spelling

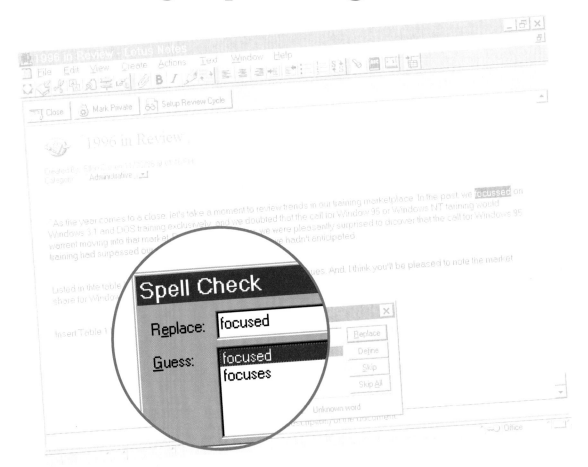

"Why would I do this?"

Checking your spelling is important, especially if you plan to share your documents with others. And, it's an easy thing to do in Notes. As you use the Spell Checker, Notes highlights words it thinks are misspelled and suggests an alternative spelling. Notes may suggest that words you use commonly are misspelled—for example, you may use an acronym for your company's name. You can add such words to the dictionary Notes uses while checking spelling.

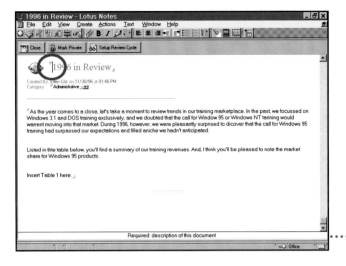

1 Open an existing document in edit mode and place the insertion point at the top of the document.

2 Open the **Edit** menu and choose the **Check Spelling** command.

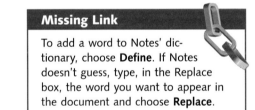

Missing Link

To add a word to Notes' dictionary, choose **Define**. If Notes doesn't guess, type, in the Replace box, the word you want to appear in the document and choose **Replace**.

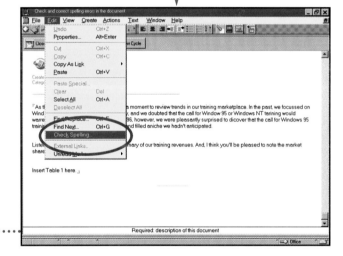

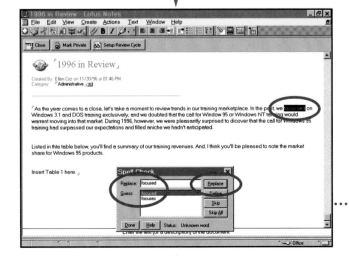

3 Notes highlights the first misspelled word it finds in your document and attempts to suggest the correct spelling. Choose a word from the **Guess** list box and then choose **Replace**.

4 Notes continues checking and identifies the next incorrectly spelled word. Again, choose a word from the **Guess** list box or choose either **Define** or **Skip**.

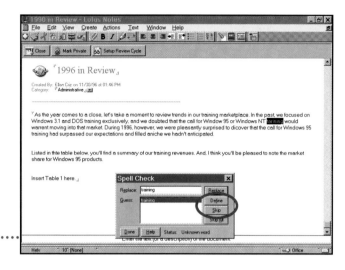

Puzzled?

If the word is spelled correctly but you don't use it often enough to add it to the Notes dictionary, choose **Skip**.

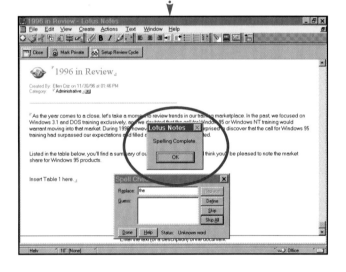

5 After Notes finishes checking your document, you'll see the dialog box in this figure. ■

Missing Link

Don't forget to save your document to keep the changes made during Spell checking.

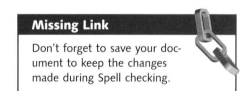

Working with Links

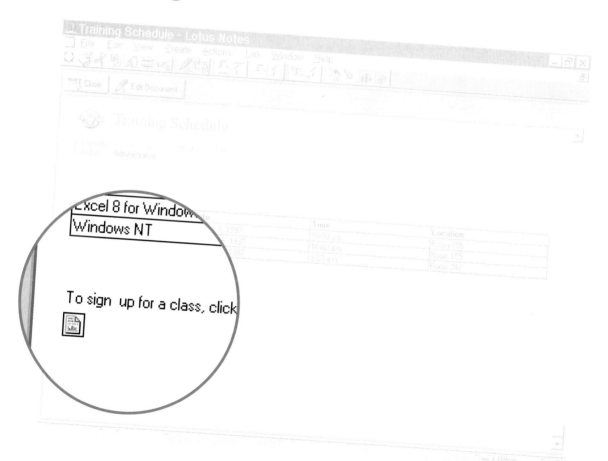

"Why would I do this?"

A link (sometimes called a DocLink) is an icon you see in database documents that switches a user from the current document to a different document, view, folder, or database in Notes. A link differs from an attachment (you learned about attachments in Part II) because an attachment switches a reader to a file created *outside* Notes. When you use a link, you stay in Notes. Suppose you want to create a link in your database that switches a user from the current document to a different document, view, folder, or database in Notes.

1 In the View pane, select the document, view, or folder you want to display when a user activates a link.

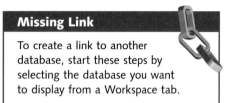

Missing Link

To create a link to another database, start these steps by selecting the database you want to display from a Workspace tab.

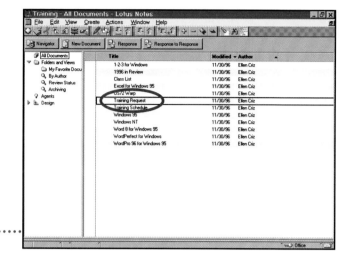

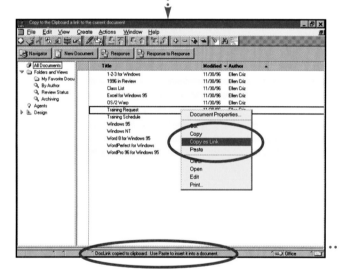

2 Click the right mouse button and choose the **Copy As Link** command from the shortcut menu. The hourglass icon appears while Notes stores the information. After the hourglass disappears, look at the center status bar at the bottom of the screen to see a message telling you that a DocLink was copied to the Clipboard.

3 Open, in edit mode, the document readers will be reading when they use the link. Place the insertion point at the spot where the link should appear, and type some text.

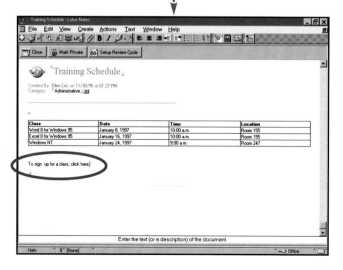

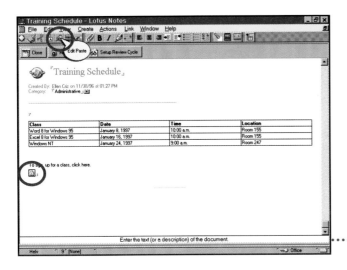

4 Click the **Paste** SmartIcon. Notes displays a link in the open document.

5 To test the link, make sure you're viewing the document that contains the link. You don't need to be in edit mode. Click the link.

Missing Link

The appearance of the link icon changes, depending on whether you linked a document, a view or folder, or a database.

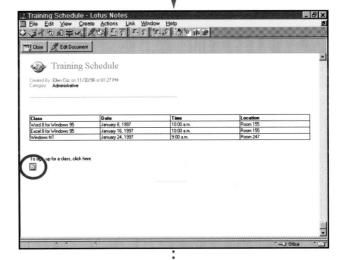

6 Notes switches to the element attached to the DocLink. To return to the original document, press **Esc**. ■

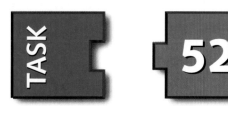

Inserting a Pop-Up Hotspot

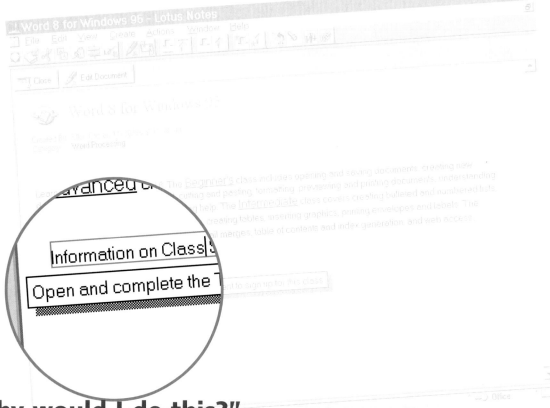

"Why would I do this?"

A hotspot is highlighted text that provides additional information or performs an action when you click it. For example, suppose you want to provide directions to a site in a document. If you put them in a hotspot, only those who need the directions can pop them up. Hotspots can perform one of four functions: provide pop-up text, go to a link, run a formula, or run a script. The last three functions are rather complex, so, in

this task, you'll learn to create and use a hotspot that provides pop-up text for the reader.

You also can enhance the hotspot using the tabs in the HotSpot Properties InfoBox. To open the HotSpot Properties InfoBox, put the document in edit mode and right-click the hotspot to display a shortcut menu. Then, choose **HotSpot Properties**.

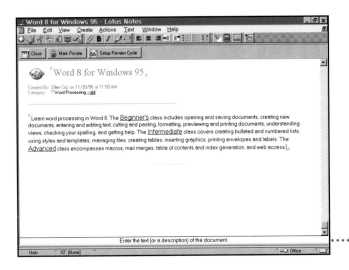

1 Open, in edit mode, the document to which you want to add a hotspot.

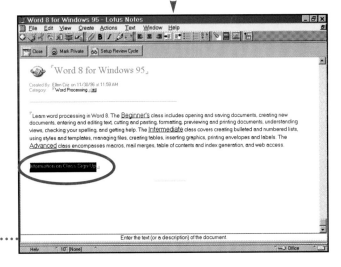

2 Type and select the text you want the reader to see that lets him know this is a pop-up. The selected text will become the pop-up.

3 Open the **Create** menu and choose **Hotspot**. From the submenu, choose **Text Pop-up**.

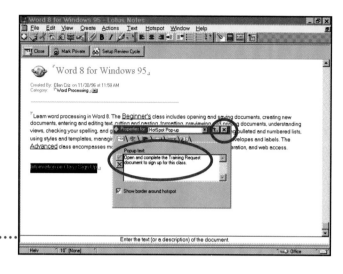

4 Notes displays the HotSpot Pop-up Properties InfoBox. In the box, type the text you want to appear when the reader clicks on the hotspot. Click the check mark to the left of the box when you finish to save the text. Click the **X** in the upper right corner to close the InfoBox.

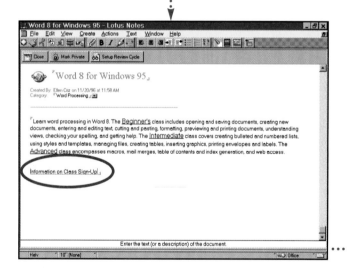

5 Notice the hotspot is highlighted in pink. Save and close the document.

6 Double-click the document in the View pane to reopen it, but not in edit mode. Click and hold the mouse button over the hotspot. ■

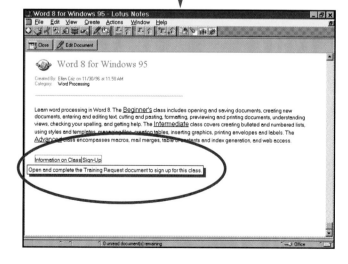

Importing Data

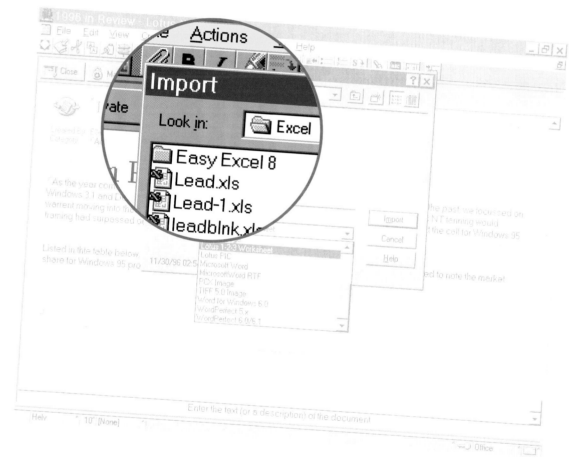

"Why would I do this?"

There are times when you'd feel more comfortable creating a document in another program, but you need the information from that document in a Notes document. You can create and save a file in another program and then import the information into a Notes document. That way, you can work in the program where you are most comfortable but still save time by not re-creating the information in Notes.

1 Open, in edit mode, the document into which you want to import information and place the insertion point at the location where you want the information to appear.

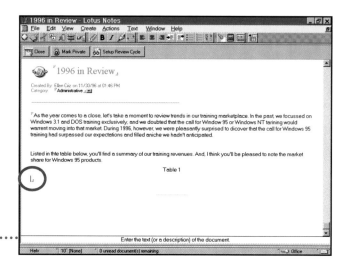

2 Open the **File** menu and choose the **Import** command. Notes displays the Import dialog box, from which you choose a document to import.

3 Navigate to the folder containing the file you want to import; highlight the file.

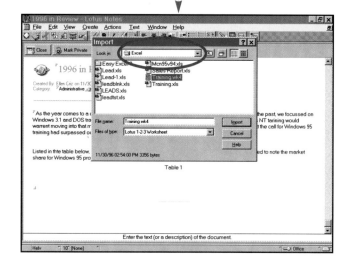

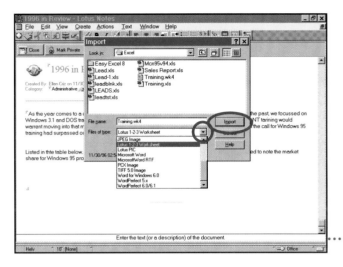

4 If Notes doesn't display the correct file type, open the **Files of type** list box and choose the type of file you intend to import. Then, choose the **Import** button.

5 The contents of the imported file appear in your Notes document. ■

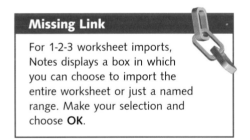

Missing Link

For 1-2-3 worksheet imports, Notes displays a box in which you can choose to import the entire worksheet or just a named range. Make your selection and choose **OK**.

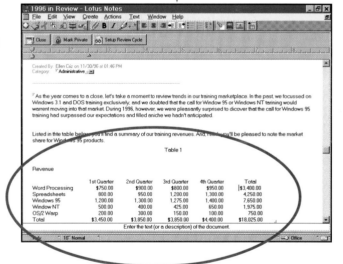

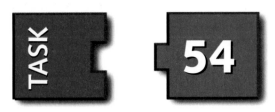

54

Creating Categories

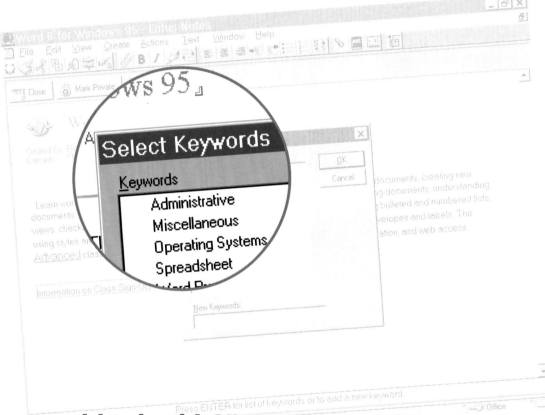

"Why would I do this?"

Many database designs include categories, which are a quick and easy way for you to organize documents in a database. If your database design includes categories, you might want to set up categories to help organize documents as you view them. The good news about categories is that you don't need special privileges to create them—for the most part, if you can create and save a document in a database, you can create and use categories.

Once you create a category, it will appear in the Select Keywords dialog box. You can select it by clicking, and Notes will place a check next to the category. You can cancel the selection of any category by clicking it a second time (to remove the check mark). You also can assign more than one category to a document by leaving multiple keywords selected.

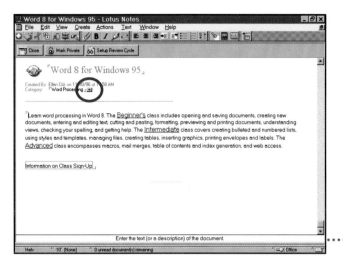

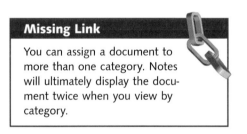

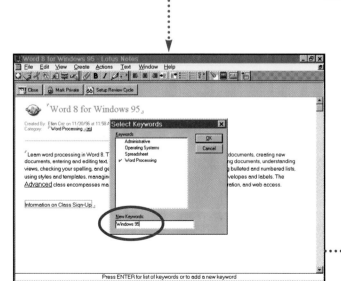

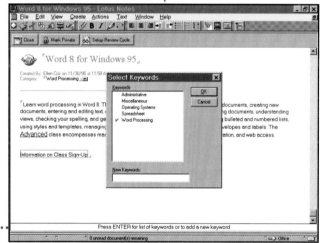

1 Open, in edit mode, the first document you want to place in a category. Click the down arrow next to the category field.

Puzzled?

If no other categories exist, the field currently contains the word Miscellaneous.

2 Notes displays the Select Keywords dialog box. If the Miscellaneous keyword is selected, click it in the list to cancel its selection.

Missing Link

You can assign a document to more than one category. Notes will ultimately display the document twice when you view by category.

3 In the New Keywords text box at the bottom of the dialog box, type the name you want to use as the category for the open document.

4 When you choose **OK**, Notes changes the category of the document to the new category you created. If you selected more than one category, each category will appear.

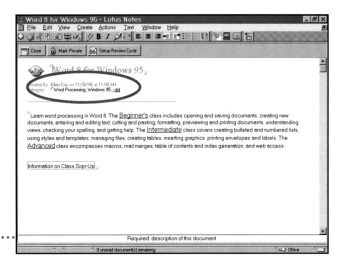

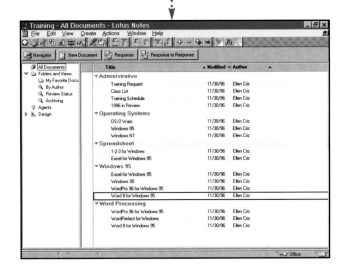

5 Save and close the document. Then, repeat these steps until you have categorized all the documents you want to categorize. ▪

Looking at Documents in Different Ways

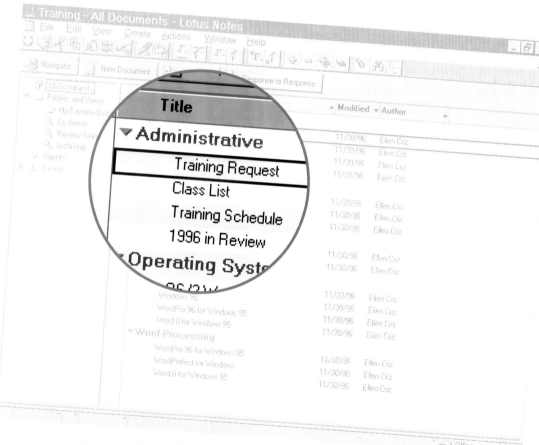

"Why would I do this?"

Once you categorize documents, you can view the documents by category, or you can tell Notes to ignore the categories and display the documents in alphabetical order by name. You also can organize documents by date—either earliest to latest or latest to earliest. And, you can do all this from within one view of the database.

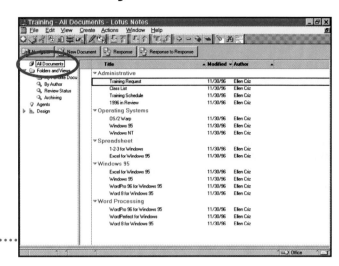

1 Open the database containing the categories you set up and select the All Documents view in the Navigation pane. In the figure, you see the documents organized by category; and the categories are in alphabetical order.

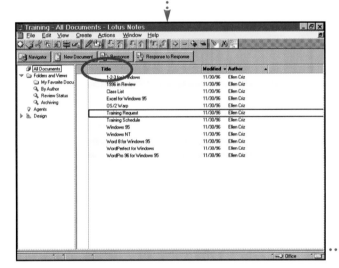

2 To hide the categories and display the documents in alphabetical order, click anywhere in the gray bar where the word Title appears.

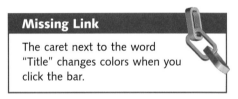

Missing Link

The caret next to the word "Title" changes colors when you click the bar.

3 To display the documents based on creation date, click the portion of the gray bar where the word Modified appears. Notes changes the order of the documents so that you view them from newest to oldest. ■

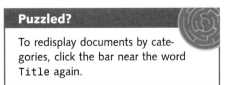

Puzzled?

To redisplay documents by categories, click the bar near the word Title again.

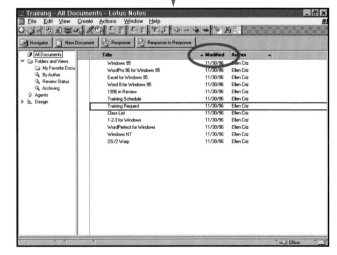

Printing Documents from a View

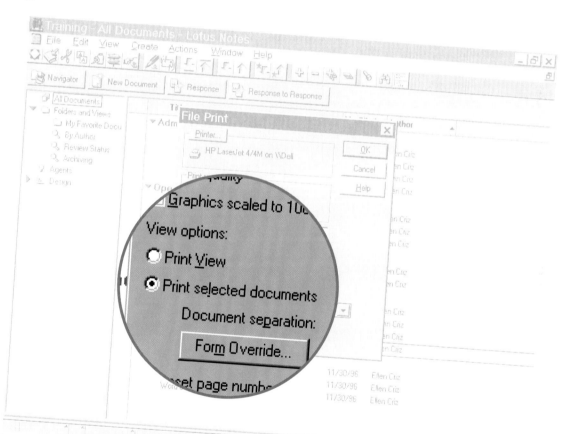

"Why would I do this?"

In Part II, you learned how to print a document (mail message) while it was open. You can, however, print a document without opening it. In fact, you can print more than one document without opening any of them.

Alternatively, you might want to print the view instead of printing documents in the view. The view provides you with the equivalent of an index of documents in the database and can serve as an easy reference tool. Alternatively, you can mark particular documents so that only their titles appear when you print the view.

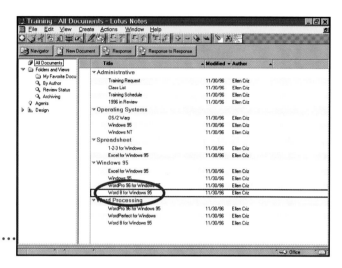

1 Highlight the view or document you want to print. To print more than one document in a view or to print the titles of only certain documents, select each by clicking in the column to the left of the document to place a check next to the document.

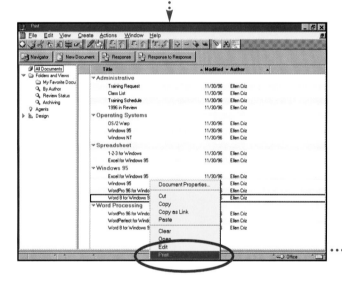

2 Press the right mouse button to display a shortcut menu. Select the **Print** command and the File Print dialog box appears.

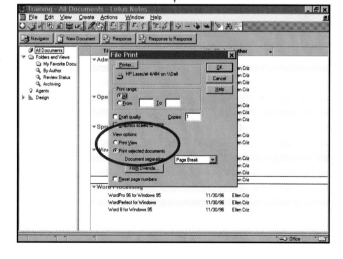

3 To print the contents of the selected document, leave the settings in the Print dialog box set to print the selected documents. To print the titles of selected documents in the view, choose **Print View**. When you choose **OK**, Notes prints the contents or the titles of the selected documents. ■

TASK

57

Removing a Database from Your Workspace

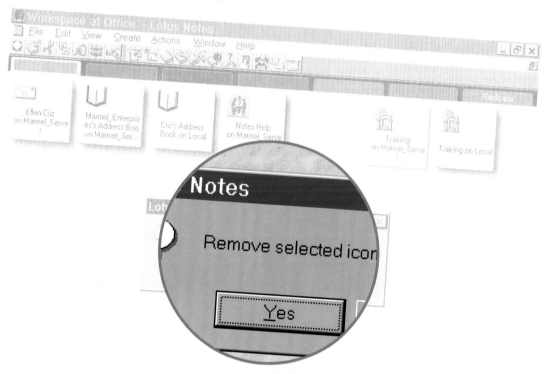

"Why would I do this?"

Once you finish working with a database, you may not want it in your Workspace any longer. You can remove the database icon from your Workspace. Removing the icon doesn't affect the database or any other Notes user. You simply can't open the database again by clicking on its icon because its icon will be gone. You can always add the icon back to your Workspace the same way you did earlier in this part.

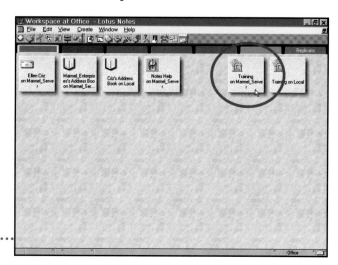

1 On the Workspace page, point at the icon for the database you want to remove.

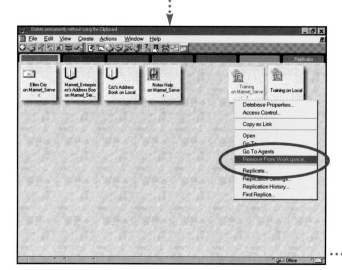

2 Click the right mouse button to display a shortcut menu and choose **Remove From Workspace**.

3 Notes displays the dialog box you see in the figure. Choose **Yes** to remove the database icon from your Workspace; choose **No** to keep the icon. ■

Puzzled?

When you remove a database from your Workspace, you aren't deleting it from your hard drive (if the database was a copy or a replica) or the server—you're simply removing the icon you use to access it.

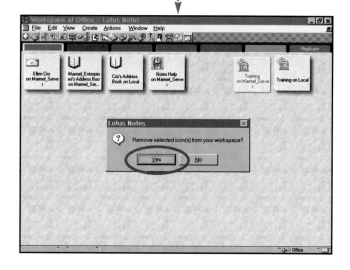

PART V

Notes and Discussion Groups

DISCUSSION GROUPS ARE ANOTHER TYPE of database in Notes. If you belong to any of the online services or you use the Internet, you may find discussion groups familiar. They are similar to newsgroups on the Internet or forums on CompuServe or America Online.

In a discussion group database, typically the documents contain information that the writer needs to share. A marketing group can share information on a marketing campaign they are developing. In many cases, the author of a document hopes to get a response to the document. For example, your company might be considering a new health benefits plan. The Health Benefits administrator might post a list of the benefits and costs associated with the new plan and then ask for reactions. You would read the document and then respond to it, and perhaps even provide reasons explaining why you feel the way you do. Your response to a document in a discussion group might prompt a third person to comment, either to the Health Benefits administrator or to you, perhaps for clarification of an issue you raise.

The point of a discussion group database is to promote communication between Notes users on issues of concern. Think of a discussion group as an informal meeting place, only you don't have to be in the same room with other people to share information and ideas. Topics for discussions are limited only by the people participating, but your company may set down some guidelines to facilitate the process, such as limiting discussion to work issues.

In discussion group databases, you'll find main topic documents, which are used to start a discussion; these documents align at the left edge of the view pane. You also see response documents; these documents are indented under the original main topic document to which they respond. Last, you'll see a "response to a response" document, which is indented below the response it answers. You can view documents organized in chronological order by date. You can also view documents by author to see what a particular person has said, or by category, which organizes main topics by subject.

Interest profiles in a discussion group database let you tell Notes about the topics, phrases, keywords, or categories that interest you so that Notes can notify you whenever an item in your interest profile appears in the topics of the database. Notes notifies you through e-mail, sending you a "newsletter" that contains a document link to the topic in the discussion group database in which you're interested.

Beginners may feel somewhat shy about participating in discussion groups—and that's okay.

You can just read information if you want; you don't need to respond. And, you can respond anonymously to a document.

Throughout this part, you'll see a sample discussion database I created based on the Discussion (R4) template that ships with Notes. You can create a database based on this template to practice, or you'll need the name of the discussion database you want to join.

TASK

58

Following the Discussion in a Discussion Group

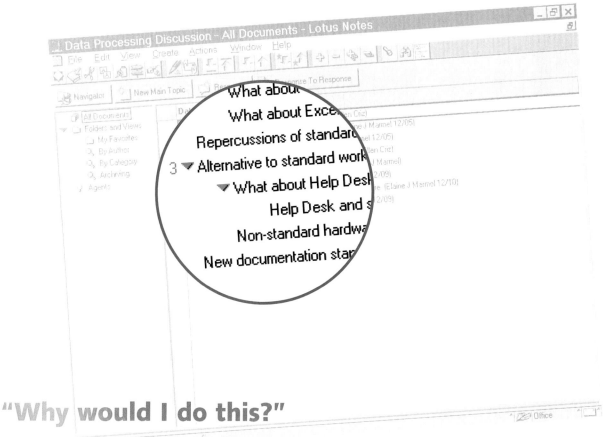

"Why would I do this?"

Joining a discussion group is nothing more than opening the appropriate Notes database. You'll find it easy to follow a discussion if you understand the views available in a discussion group database. In this task, you'll explore the views in a Discussion database. You'll see that main topics align with the left edge of the view, while responses appear indented below the document

to which they respond. Response to response documents appear indented below the document they answer. In the figures in this task, "What about Help Desk?," is a response to a main topic document, "Alternative to standard workstation." "Help Desk and standard software" is a response to response document that answers "What about Help Desk?".

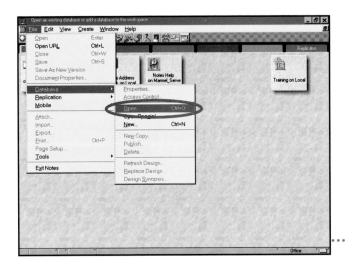

1 Open the **File** menu and choose the **Database** command. From the submenu, choose **Open**.

2 Notes displays the Open Database dialog box. In the Server list box, choose the server containing the discussion group you want to join and highlight the database. Highlight the discussion database you want to use and click **Open**.

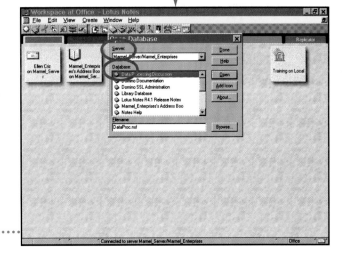

3 Notes adds an icon to your Workspace tab and opens the database. You'll see the About this Database document. In this case, it describes how discussion groups work. Press **Esc**, or open the **File** menu and choose the **Close** command.

4 The views for the database appear. In the default view, the All Documents view, four main topic documents appear in chronological order from earliest to latest. In the Navigation pane, click **By Category**.

> **Puzzled?**
>
> If you created your own discussion database, it will probably be empty. Documents appear in the example to make this discussion more clear.

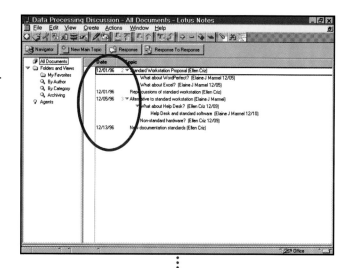

5 The documents are re-displayed by subject. This figure shows two categories: Documentation and Workstation. In the Navigation pane, click **By Author**.

> **Missing Link**
>
> Only main topic documents can be categorized; all responses and response to responses assume the category of the main topic document.

6 The documents are re-organized by the names of the people who wrote them. ■

> **Missing Link**
>
> When you use the Author view, you don't see the hierarchy that indicates whether a document is a main topic, response, or response to response.

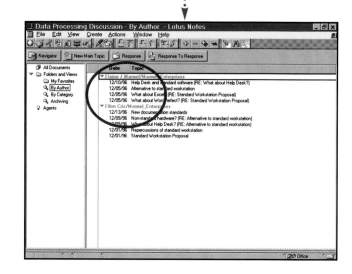

Posting a Message in a Discussion Group

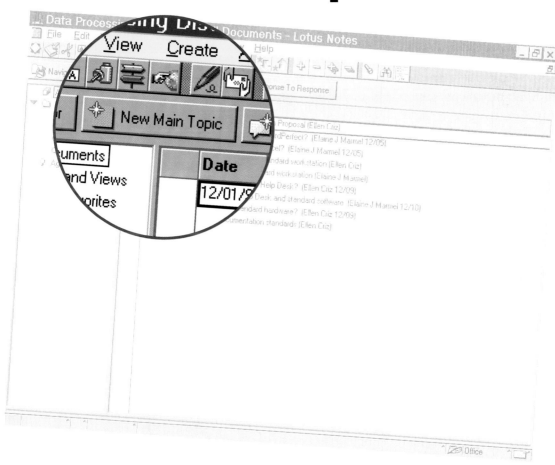

"Why would I do this?"

Posting a message in a discussion group is the same as creating a new document in any other database. In this task, you'll learn how to create a document that starts a new main topic for discussion. As you would expect, the title of the document will be the topic you see in the View pane. And, you can categorize main topic documents.

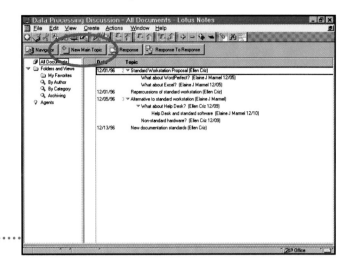

1 Open the Discussion database to any view you choose. Click the **New Main Topic** button in the Action bar.

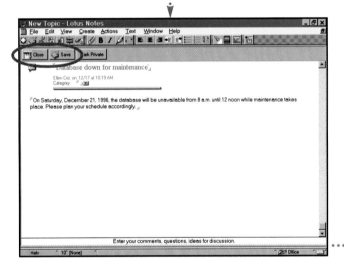

2 In the document window, fill in the information you want to store in the document. To categorize the document, open the category list box and either choose a category or type a new one. Click **Save** and **Close** in the Action bar.

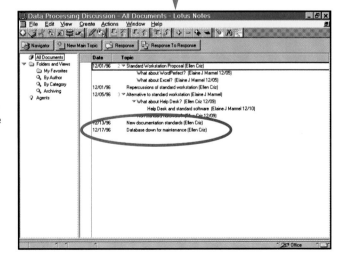

3 Your new main topic document appears, in chronological order, aligned at the left edge of the topic column. ■

Reading and Responding to a Main Topic Document

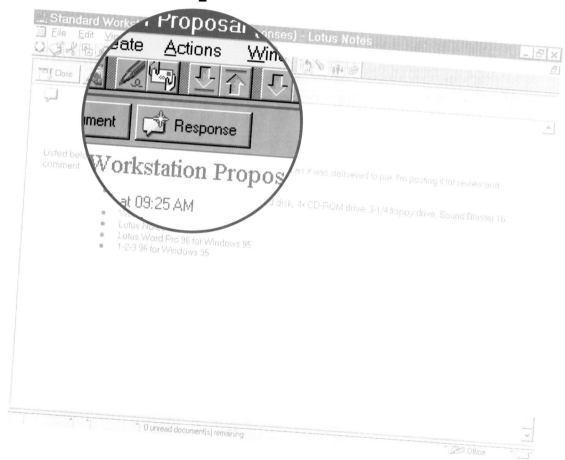

"Why would I do this?"

Suppose you read a main topic document and you'd like to add to the discussion. You can create a response document either while reading a main topic document or from the View pane. In this task, you'll create a response document while viewing a main topic document; that way, you can read all the information in the main topic document before creating an answer.

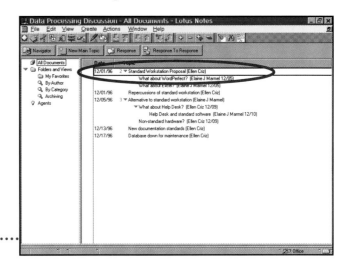

1 In the View pane, identify the main topic document you want to read and double-click it.

2 Notes opens the document so that you can read it.

Missing Link

If you already know the content of the main document, you can, instead, highlight the main topic in the view and click the Response button in the Action bar to directly open a response document. If you choose this approach, skip Step 3.

3 After reading the document, click the **Response** button in the Action bar to open a response document.

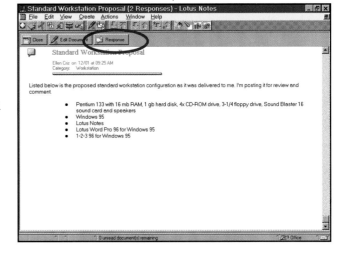

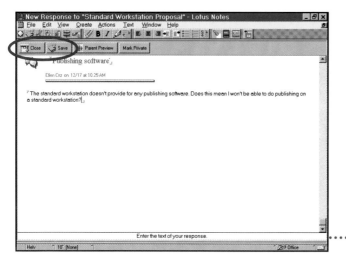

4 Type your response; then click the **Save** and **Close** buttons on the Action bar or press **Esc** and choose **Yes** to save and close the document.

5 After closing the document, Notes redisplays the main topic document. Click **Close** on the Action bar.

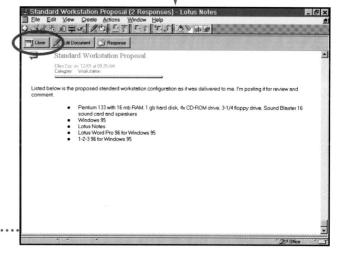

Puzzled?

If you chose to open a response document directly in Step 2, Notes skips this step.

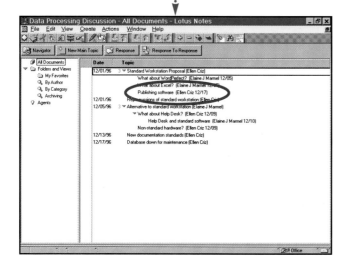

6 In the View pane, your response appears indented below the main topic document to which you responded. ■

Responding to a Response Document

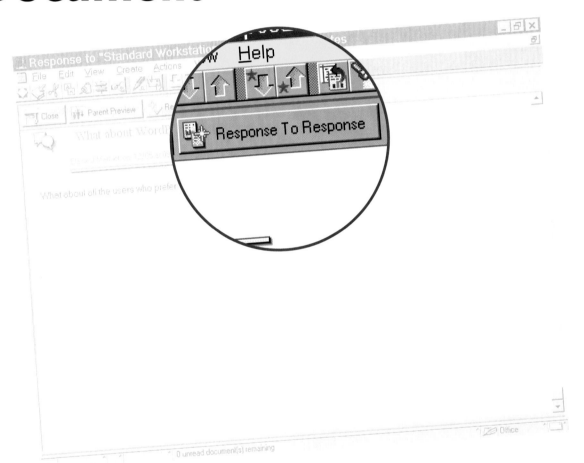

"Why would I do this?"

Suppose you find a response document someone created and you want to comment on that
document. Then, you create a "response to a
response" document. Like response documents,
you can create this document either while reading a response or from the View pane.

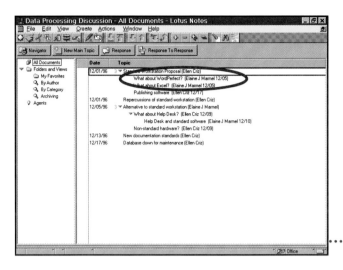

1 In the View pane, identify the response document you want to read and double-click it.

2 Notes opens the document so that you can read it.

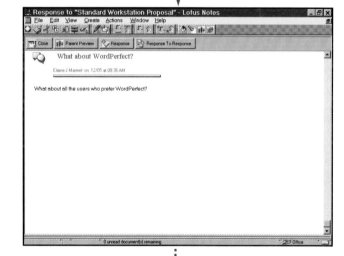

Missing Link

If you already know the content of the response document, you can, instead, click the Response To Response button in the action bar to directly open a response to response document. If you choose this approach, skip Step 3.

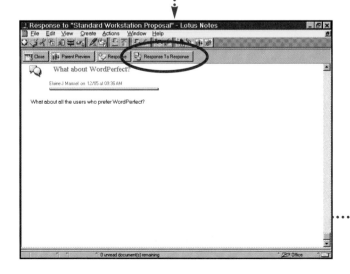

3 After reading the document, click the **Response To Response** button in the Action bar to open a response document.

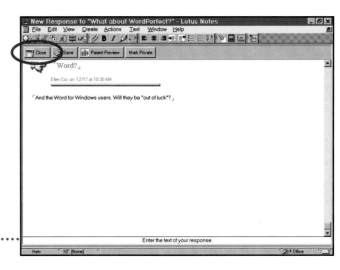

4 Type your response; click the **Save** and **Close** buttons on the Action bar.

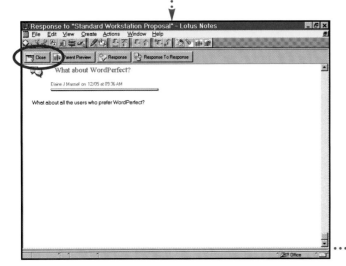

5 After closing the document, Notes redisplays the Response document. Click the **Close** button on the Action bar.

Puzzled?

If you chose to open a response to response document directly in Step 2, Notes skips this step.

6 In the View pane, your response appears indented below the response document that you answered. ■

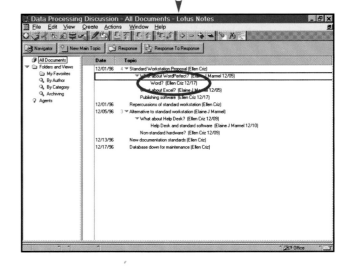

Responding Anonymously

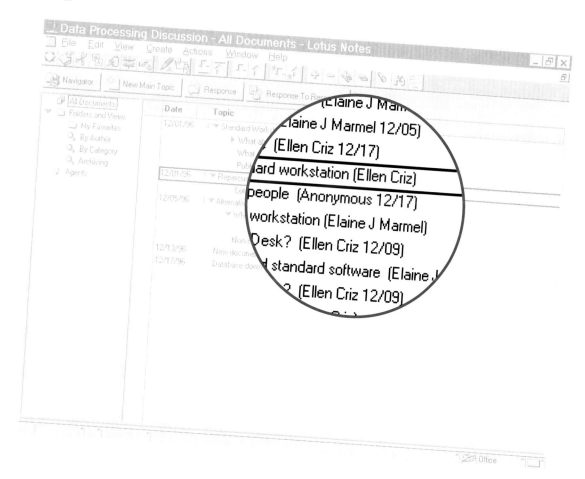

"Why would I do this?"

Suppose you want to respond, but you don't want anybody to know that you're the person responding. Maybe the topic is highly sensitive, or maybe you're just shy. You can create either a response document or a response to a response document that keeps your identity anonymous.

Be aware that the database designer may have disabled anonymous responding, so this function might not be available.

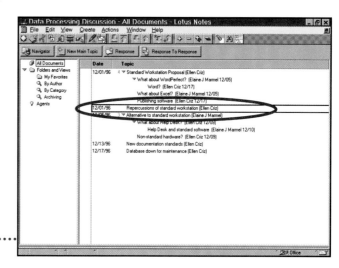

1 Highlight the document to which you want to create an anonymous response (or response to response).

2 Open the **Create** menu and choose **Other**.

3 In the Other dialog box, choose the type of anonymous document you want to create. Choose **OK**.

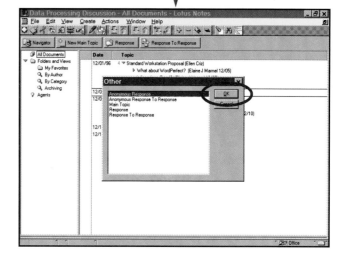

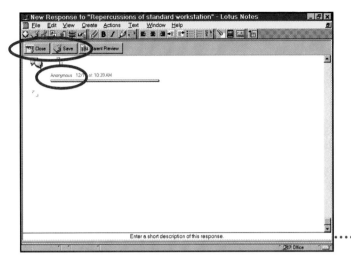

4 Notes displays a document similar to the one you see in this figure, where the author is Anonymous. Complete the document; then click the **Save** and **Close** buttons on the Action bar.

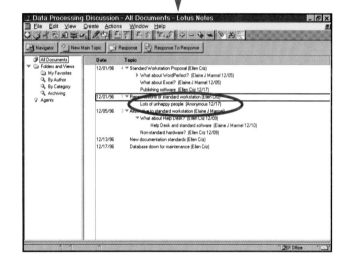

5 The View pane reappears. Your document, with an author of Anonymous, appears below the document to which you responded. ■

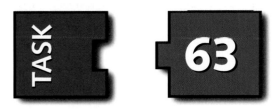

Letting Notes Find Topics That Interest You

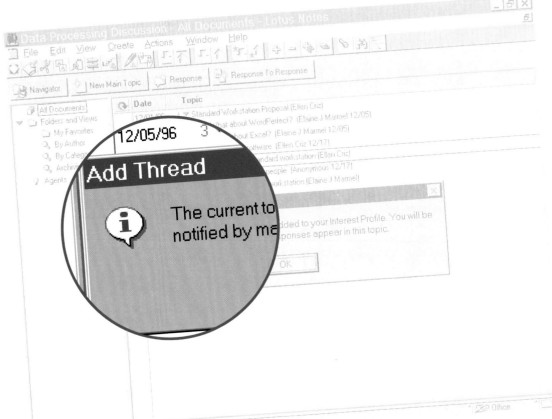

"Why would I do this?"

You can let Notes help you find topics in a discussion database that are of particular interest to you. To let Notes do the work, set up an interest profile, in which you identify information you want Notes to watch for in the database. In the interest profile, you can ask Notes to inform you about new documents that contain your name, are written by a particular author, appear in particular categories, or contain certain words or phrases. When Notes comes across a document that meets your criteria, Notes notifies you via e-mail. And, you can monitor a particular discussion thread (main topic and responses) by adding that thread to your interest profile.

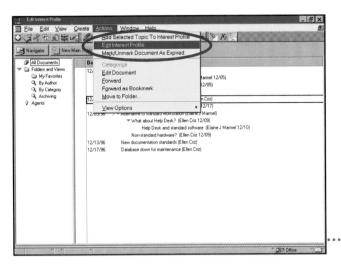

1 Open the Discussion database; then open the **Actions** menu and choose **Edit Interest Profile**.

2 Enter your interests in the brackets and save and close the document.

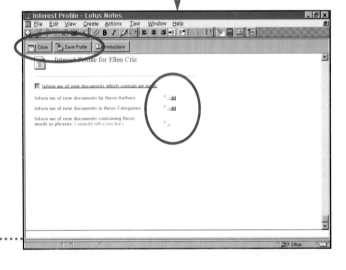

3 To add a discussion thread to your interest profile, highlight the document that begins that thread. Open the **Actions** menu and choose **Add Selected Topic To Interest Profile**.

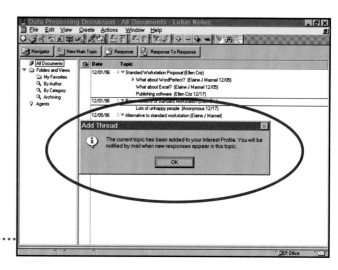

4 Notes informs you after adding the thread that you'll be notified by mail of new responses. Click **OK**.

5 Your interest profile is added to the view. Double-click it to reopen it.

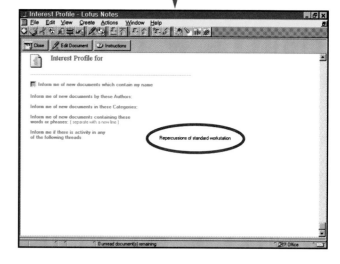

6 You'll see the topic of the thread you just added at the bottom of the profile. ■

PART VI

Notes and Traveling

UNTIL NOW, WE'VE VIRTUALLY IGNORED the fact that you can continue to use Notes while you're away from the office. Actually, the way you use Notes while you're not in the office depends on whether you travel with or without a computer. If you travel without a computer, you can handle things in one of two ways: you can allow someone to handle your mail and your calendar for you while you're away, or you can have

Notes inform anyone who sends you mail that you're away. By the way, if someone asks you to handle her mail and calendar for her while she is away, you'll have no trouble; you can handle the job right from your own computer.

On the other hand, if you travel with a computer, you can continue to use Notes from that computer. To take this concept a step further, you even can use Notes from the computer you have at home. The point is, Notes can be available to you from *any* computer, not just the one on your desk at work.

The computer from which you use Notes is referred to as the Notes Client machine; you connect that machine to a server, which manages all the activities you do while working in Notes. The server puts your mail in your mailbox, and the databases you access are stored on the server. While you work in the office, your client machine typically connects to the server through your company's network. When you're away from the office, your client machine typically uses a modem to connect to the server. A modem is a piece of hardware that works with a telephone to connect one computer to another, remote computer. When you connect this way, you're using a "dial-up" connection.

It's important to understand that you can do the same work in Notes whether you use a dial-up connection or whether you connect in your office over the network. The only difference is how you connect. If you use a notebook computer while you're away from the office, you should test your connection before you actually go on the road; just complete Tasks 66–68 in this part and then use a phone line in your office to dial into the server. That way, you'll know that "everything works" before you leave town.

If you want to work on a database while you're away from the office, you should copy all or part of that database to your client machine before you go on the road. That way, you can work offline, without connecting to the server. By working offline, you can make changes and create documents without running up a phone bill. When you make this special local copy of a database, the local copy is called a local replica, and you can use a local replica whether you're at the office or on the road.

In Part IV, you learned to make a local copy of a database. You may be wondering about the difference between a local copy and a local replica. You create a local copy of a database when you intend to use it exclusively on your computer, and you don't intend to send changes to the database back to the server. You might recall the example used in Part IV of a company forms database. In this example, I suggested that you might want to copy the forms database to your machine to use, but you wouldn't make changes to the forms and send them back to the server. You'd just use them at your machine. When you want to share changes to a database by sending them back to a server, you use a replica. And,

for those of you who care about how Notes knows the difference between a copy and a replica, Notes assigns IDs to each database you create. When you create a new local copy, Notes assigns a unique ID, but when you create a replica, Notes assigns to the replica the same ID the database has on the server.

When you finish working offline, you connect your client machine to the server and send the changes in your local replica to the database on the server. You use a process called replication to send the changes. When Notes replicates, it figures out what changes you have made and incorporates that information into the database on the server without making changes to any other information in the database. Replication is a two-way process; the server receives the changes you made and, if you want, will send you new changes made by others since the last time you replicated.

TASK

64

Letting Someone Else Handle Your Mail

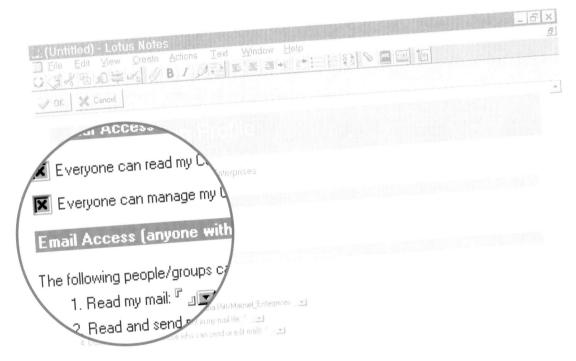

"Why would I do this?"

If you don't travel with a computer, you can let someone else handle your Notes e-mail for you while you're away from the office. To give someone access to your Mail database, you must include him or her on your Delegation Profile. You can display and modify the Delegation Profile from either the Workspace or from inside your Mail database—the steps are the same. However, if you perform this task from the Workspace, your Mail database must be selected.

On the Delegation Profile, you can allow people to read your mail, read and respond to your mail, read, edit and send any document in your Mail database, and delete mail. You can give different people different privileges, and you don't have to provide all privileges to anyone. However, anyone who gets access to your e-mail, even just to read it, also gets access to your Calendar. So, don't forget to edit your Delgation Profile again when you return to the office.

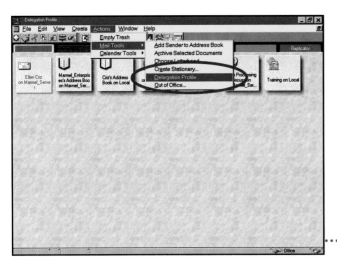

1 Open the **Actions** menu and highlight the **Mail Tools** command. From the cascading menu that appears, choose **Delegation Profile**.

Puzzled?

From the Workspace, click the **Mail** database first; otherwise, you won't see the Mail Tools command on the Action menu.

2 In the Email Access section of the Delegation Profile, supply the names of those people to whom you want to give access to your e-mail. Click **OK** when you finish. To access a mailbox for which you are a delegate, choose **Actions**, **Calendar Tools**, **Open Another Calendar**. From the Address Book, choose the person whose mailbox you want to open.

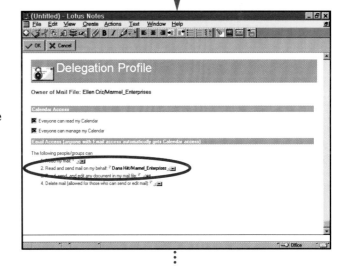

Missing Link

Use the list box arrow to display the Address Book and choose people. Choose **OK** when you finish using the Address Book.

3 Notes displays the Mailbox of the person you selected. In the figure, you're no longer looking at Ellen Criz's mailbox; instead, you're looking at my mailbox. Click the **Inbox** to see her mail. ■

Missing Link

To close a delegated mailbox, choose **File**, **Close**. You also can switch back and forth between your own mailbox and the delegated mailbox by opening the **Window** menu and choosing the appropriate Mail database.

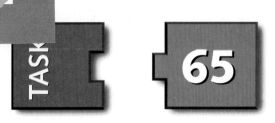

TASK 65

Sending "Out of the Office" Message Replies

"Why would I do this?"

If you don't travel with a computer and you don't want to let someone else handle your e-mail, you can use the Out of Office Profile to let Notes send a reply automatically to any message you receive while you're gone—and the reply will explain that you are away and provide a date when you will return. Notes will send only one message to any person, even if you receive several messages from the same person. When you return to the office, Notes will send you a "Welcome Back" message that

lists all the people who received your "Out of Office" message. Until you disable the Out of Office agent, Notes will continue to send you "Welcome Back" messages.

You can open the Out of Office Profile from either the Workspace or from inside your Mail database—the steps are the same. However, if you perform this task from the Workspace, your Mail database must be selected.

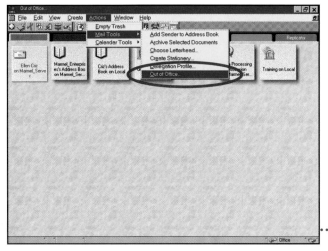

1 Open the **Actions** menu and highlight the **Mail Tools** command. From the cascading menu that appears, choose **Out of Office**.

> **Puzzled?**
>
> From the Workspace, click the **Mail** database first; otherwise, you won't see the Mail Tools command on the Action menu.

2 Provide the date you are leaving and the date you will return. If you want, change the text in the message Notes will send. Also, if you want, specify a group of people who should receive a different message and type that message. When you finish, click **Enable Out of Office Agent**. Notes may ask you to choose a server; choose your Mail server.

> **Missing Link**
>
> At the bottom of the form, you can specify people to whom Notes shouldn't respond at all. And clicking Close sets up the profile but doesn't tell Notes to start answering messages for you.

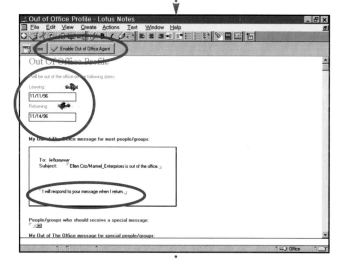

3 When you return to the office and no longer want Notes to respond to your messages, choose **Actions**, **Mail Tools**, **Out of Office**, and click the **I Have Returned to the Office** button on the Action bar. Notes displays a "Welcome Back" message, in which you choose **OK**. ■

Setting Up Your Modem for Travel

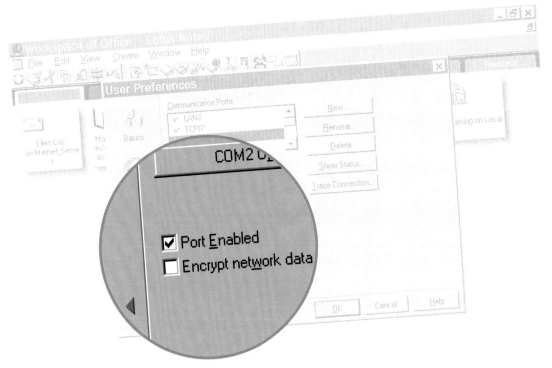

"Why would I do this?"

There are a few things you should do to set up the computer on which you'll use Notes away from the office (the client machine). You'll need a modem installed in your computer, and you'll also need to set up a Location document that describes the connection settings you want to use. To set up your modem in Notes, you'll need to know the port your modem uses. On computers using a serial mouse, your mouse usually uses COM1, and your modem usually uses

COM2. You may need to check with your administrator for help identifying your modem port.

When you enable a port for a modem, Notes will add that port to all your location documents. You may want to edit other location documents (such as Office or Island) and remove the check from the port check box. To edit each location document, choose **File**, **Mobile**, **Locations**. Highlight a location document and click the **Edit Location** button on the Action bar.

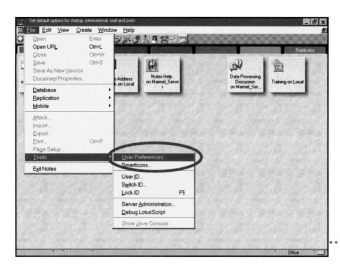

1 Open the **File** menu and choose **Tools**. From the submenu, choose **User Preferences**.

2 In the left side of the User Preferences dialog box, choose **Ports**. In the Communication Ports list, make sure a check mark appears next to the port on which your modem is installed. If you don't see a check mark, highlight the port and choose the **Port Enabled** checkbox to place a check in it.

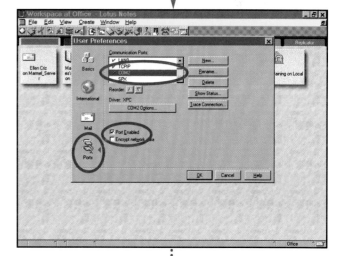

Missing Link

Remember, Notes enables this port for all locations. Don't forget to edit the appropriate location documents and disable the port.

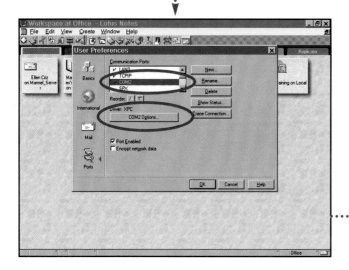

3 (Optional) If you need to select a modem or want to hear the phone dialing when you call into the server, highlight your modem port (for example, COM2) and click the **Options** button for your modem port to display the Additional Setup dialog box.

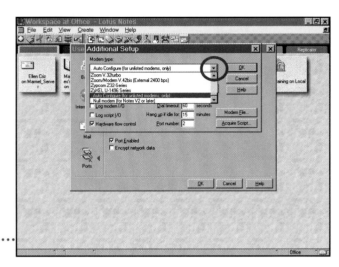

4 To select a modem, open the **Modem type** list box and choose your modem. If your modem doesn't appear in the list, use either the default of Auto Configure and let Notes set up your modem or try Generic All-Speed Modem File.

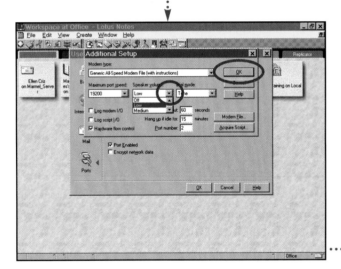

5 If you want to hear your modem, change the Speaker Volume to Low, Medium, or High (Low is usually sufficient). Choose **OK** to close the Additional Setup dialog box and redisplay the User Preferences dialog box.

6 Choose **OK** to close the User Preferences dialog box.

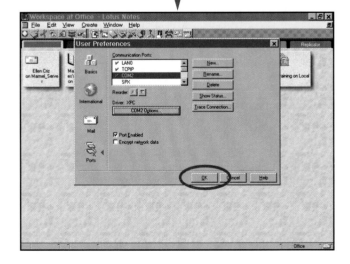

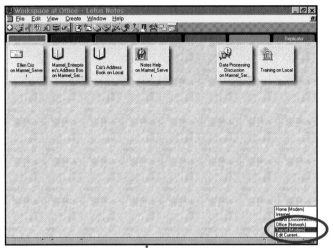

7 In the lower right portion of the status bar, click the box that currently displays Office. Notes displays a pop-up menu. Choose **Travel (Modem)** to use the Travel location settings.

Missing Link

Each location corresponds to a location document that describes the settings you want to use to connect to the server. If you're working from home, choose **Home (Modem)**.

8 Notes displays the Time and Phone Information for Travel dialog box. Use this dialog box to enter phone (including outside line, country, and area codes), date, and time information before making a call. Choose **OK**. To view the Travel location settings, open the **File** menu and choose **Mobile**. From the submenu, choose **Edit Current Location**.

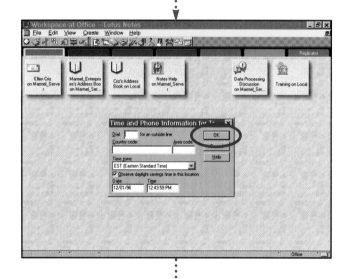

Missing Link

You can also view the settings of the current location by clicking the pop-up box on the status bar and choosing **Edit Current...**.

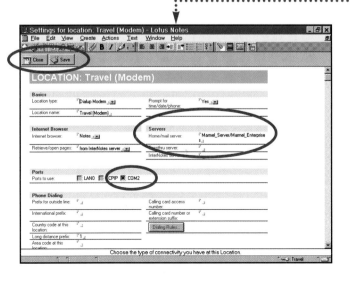

9 Your Travel Location document should look similar to the one in the figure. Make sure that your modem port is checked and that your server and domain name appear in the Home/mail server field. To save changes, click **Save** and then **Close** in the Action bar. You may see the Time and Phone Information for Travel dialog box again—click **OK**. ■

67

Setting Up the Server Phone Number

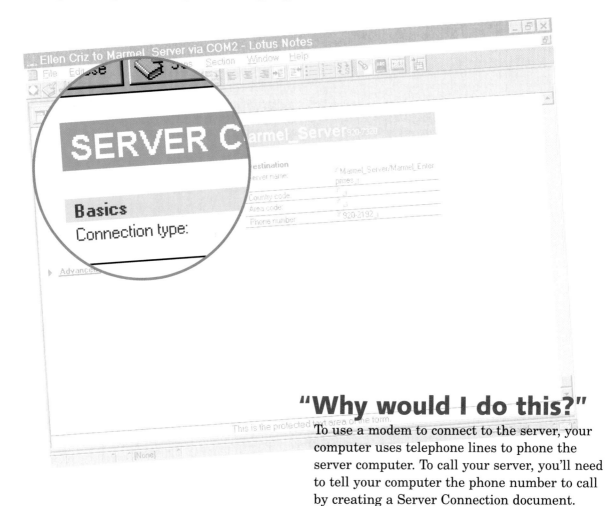

"Why would I do this?"

To use a modem to connect to the server, your computer uses telephone lines to phone the server computer. To call your server, you'll need to tell your computer the phone number to call by creating a Server Connection document.

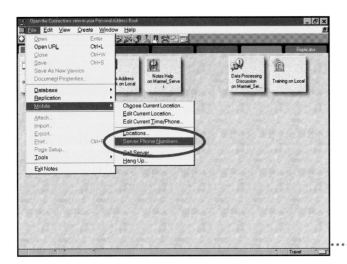

1 Open the **File** menu and choose **Mobile**. From the submenu, choose **Server Phone Numbers**.

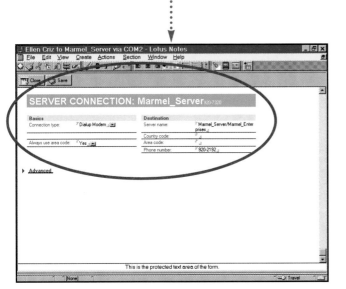

2 Click the **Add Connection** button.

3 Fill in the Connection document so that it resembles the one you see in the figure—using your own Server name, Country code, Area code, and Phone number. Click **Save** and **Close** in the Action bar. ■

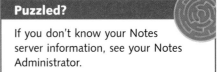

Puzzled?

If you don't know your Notes server information, see your Notes Administrator.

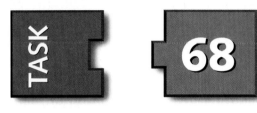

Taking a Database on the Road

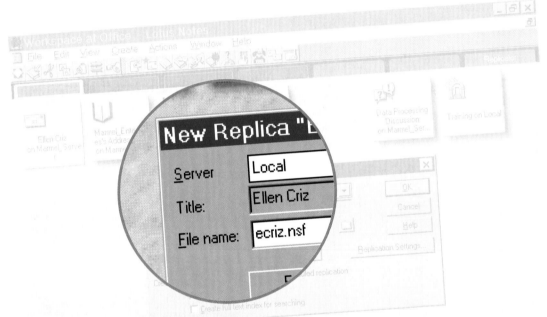

"Why would I do this?"

Suppose you want to make changes to a database or answer mail while you're away from the office. Before you travel, you'll want to place all, or a part of, that database on the computer you use away from the office so you can work offline. To make a local database that you can change and later send those changes to the server, you create a local replica of the database. Let's replicate your mail database onto the notebook computer with which you intend to travel. During replication, Notes creates a temporary database icon; when replication finishes, Notes deletes that icon and converts the original

icon into a *stacked* icon that you can use to open either the database on the server or the local replica.

To perform this task, you must use your notebook computer at your office and connect it to the server through your company's network. If your notebook computer doesn't contain a network card (or if you're working from a home desktop computer), you can't connect to the server through your company's network. Instead, you'll need to connect the client to the server via modem and replicate a database from the server via modem. See Task 69 to learn how.

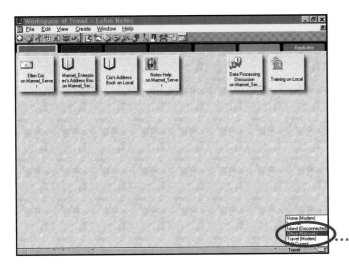

1 (Optional) On your notebook computer, in your Workspace, if you see Travel (Modem) in the box on the lower right portion of the status bar, click the box. Choose Office (Network) to connect to your server through your company network.

2 In your Workspace, click the database for which you want to create a local replica. Then, open the **File** menu, choose **Replication**, and from the submenu, choose **New Replica**.

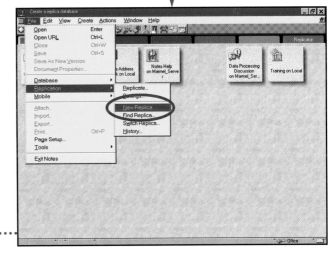

Missing Link

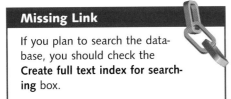

If you plan to search the database, you should check the **Create full text index for searching** box.

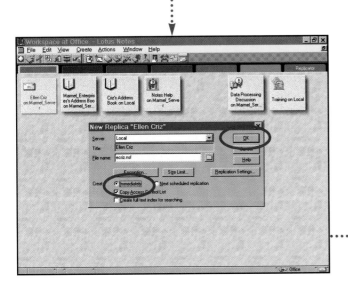

3 In the New Replica dialog box, make sure the Server is set to Local. Choose the **Immediately** option button and then choose **OK**.

Missing Link

To limit the size of the replica, select **Size Limit** and specify, in gigabytes, the size for the replica. To replicate only part of the database, choose **Replication Settings** and specify the settings you want to use during replication.

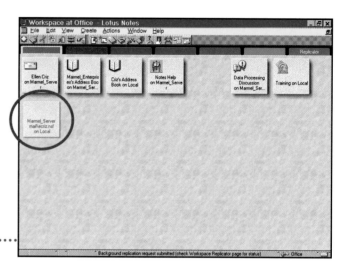

4 Notes places a new temporary database icon on the Workspace tab, but it doesn't contain a picture (like the letter for a mail database) because Notes has not finished replicating the database, as indicated by the message in the status bar. Click the **Replicator** tab to watch replication.

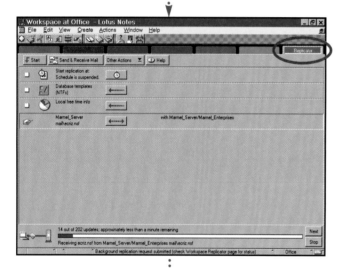

5 When Notes finishes replicating, you'll see a message in the status bar at the bottom of the screen for a message indicating that replication is finished. Click the Workspace tab containing the database.

Puzzled?

If you have previously replicated the selected database, Notes displays a box asking if you want to replace it. Choose **Yes** to replace it or **No** to return to the New Replica dialog box.

6 The temporary database icon is gone and Notes turns the original database icon into a stacked icon—one you can use to access either the local replica or the database on the server. Use the down arrow on that stacked database icon to choose a database to open. ■

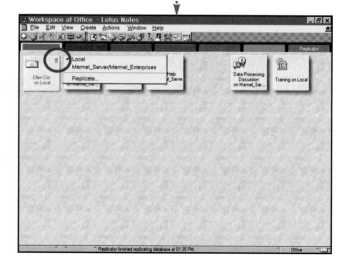

Connecting While on the Road

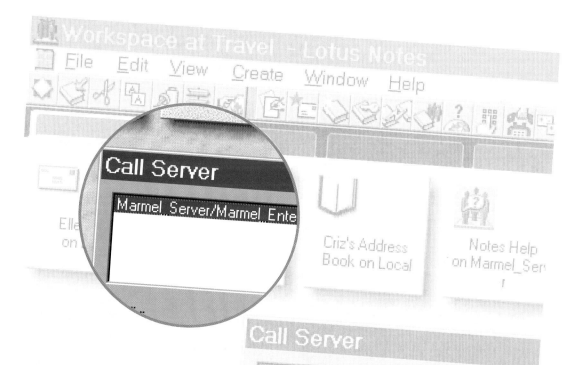

"Why would I do this?"

At the office, chances are good that your network automatically connects your computer to the server. Now, learn how to connect to the server using a modem. For these steps to work, you must have completed the steps in all the previous tasks in Part VI. If you're planning to use Notes on a notebook computer, you can connect your notebook computer to your server

via a telephone line and perform the steps in this task in the office to test and make sure your connection will work.

If you see Office in the box on the lower right portion of the status bar, click the box. Notes displays a pop-up menu. Choose **Travel (Modem)** to change to the Travel location.

1 As you switch to the Travel location, Notes displays the Time and Phone Information for Travel dialog box. Complete the information necessary to initiate a phone call from your current location. For example, if you need to dial 9 to get an outside line, enter that in the Dial text box. Then choose **OK**. Open the **File** menu and choose **Mobile**. From the submenu, choose **Call Server**.

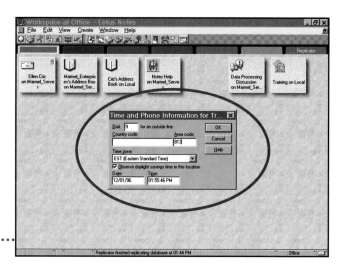

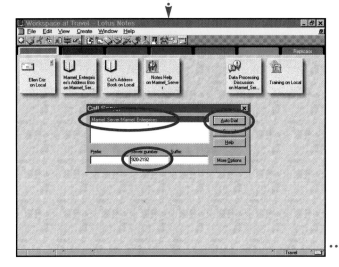

Missing Link

When you get back to the office, don't forget to change the location back to Office.

2 In the Call Server dialog box, highlight the server you want to call and choose **Auto Dial**. Notes dials your server. Watch your status bar to see when you are connected.

3 To hang up from the server, open the **File** menu and choose **Mobile**. From the submenu, choose **Hang Up**. The Hang Up dialog box appears. Click **Hang Up**. ■

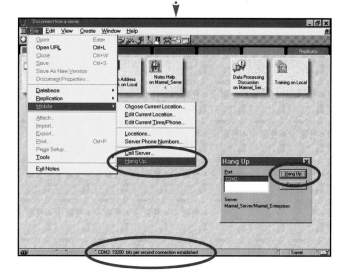

Sending and Receiving Mail on the Road

"Why would I do this?"

While you're on the road, sending and receiving electronic mail is an easy and efficient way to stay in touch with others and get things done. When you send mail while traveling, Notes sends the mail in your local Mail database to the server; if you receive mail, you'll see it in the Inbox of your local Mail database. When Notes finishes sending and receiving mail, it updates the Replicator tab of your Workspace with information on the messages sent and received and then automatically hangs up the call.

Task 70: Sending and Receiving Mail on the Road

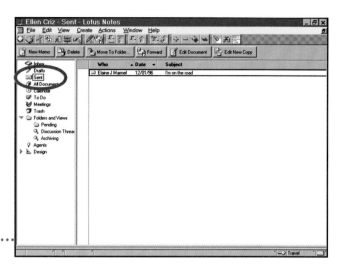

1 Open your local Mail database and create any mail you need to send. When you finish a document, choose **Send** or **Send and File**. The mail will appear in the Sent view of your Mail database. Close your Mail database when you finish.

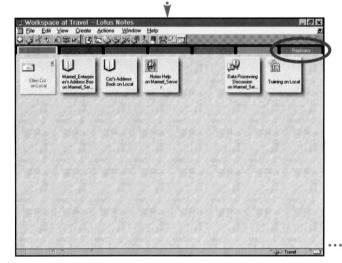

Puzzled?

If this is the first time you have opened your local Mail database, you will see the About Mail document. Press **Esc** to close it.

2 Click the **Replicator** tab on your Workspace.

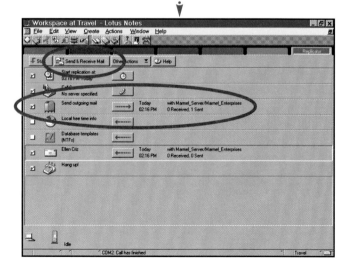

3 Click the **Send & Receive Mail** button. Notes calls your server. Watch the bottom of the screen and the status line for information on the progress of connecting. ■

Uploading Changes to Databases

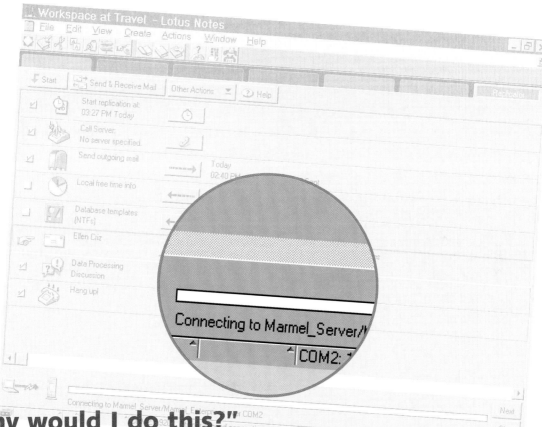

Connecting to Marmel_Server/I

COM2: 1

Connecting to Marmel_Server/Marmel_Enter... COM2

...d connection established

"Why would I do this?"

Here's the scenario: you went on the road and took a local replica database with you. You opened the database, and you made changes to the database—maybe you added a document like we did. You saved the document and closed the database. Now, you need to upload the changes you made to the server by replicating your database onto the server. When you replicate the database, Notes is smart enough to incorporate your changes into the database without changing documents that you didn't modify.

When Notes finishes replicating the database, it updates the Replicator tab of your Workspace and automatically hangs up the call. By the way, when you get back to the office, don't forget to change the location back to Office; you can use the pop-up on the status bar.

201

Task 71: Uploading Changes to Databases

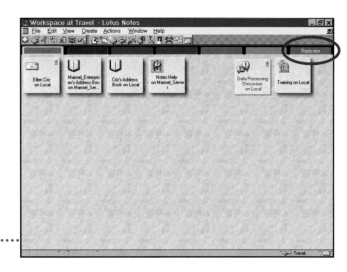

1 Click the **Replicator** tab on your Workspace.

2 To both send and receive updates, click the arrow next to the database you intend to replicate. Notes displays a dialog box you can use to both send and receive documents. Make sure check marks appear in both checkboxes and choose **OK**.

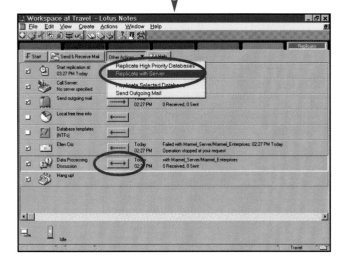

3 Notice the arrow changes to a double-headed arrow. Click the **Other Actions** button and choose **Replicate with Server**.

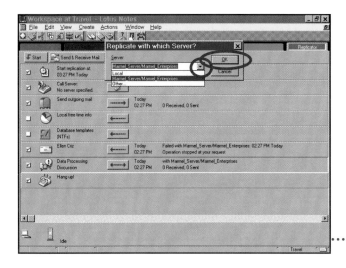

4 From the Server list box, choose the server to which you want to send changes. Choose **OK**.

5 Notes uses the telephone lines to call your server. Watch the bottom of the screen and the status line for information on the progress of connecting.

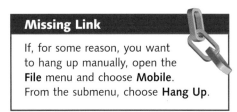

Missing Link

If, for some reason, you want to hang up manually, open the **File** menu and choose **Mobile**. From the submenu, choose **Hang Up**.

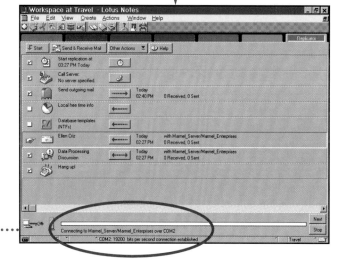

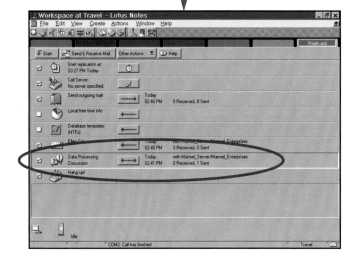

6 When replication finishes, Notes hangs up and updates the Replicator tab of the Workspace. ∎

PART VII

Setting Notes Preferences

IN PART VII, YOU LEARN HOW to customize your Notes Workspace. You can, for example, set options that tell Notes when to empty trash and actually delete documents you have marked for deletion. You also have the option to keep copies of the mail you send.

Another easy way to customize your Workspace is to place text labels on the folder tabs of your Workspace to help you organize your Notes databases. Once you have labeled the Workspace tabs, you can move databases back and forth from one tab to another. Keeping similar databases grouped together makes data easier to find.

As part of the actions you take to customize your Workspace, you should change your password. Most system administrators set user passwords to some default value, and encourage users to change their passwords as soon as they can. Notes makes it easy for you to change your personal password whenever you like.

Last, as promised in the beginning of the book, at the end of this part, you will learn how to change the appearance of the database icons and the Workspace background. When you first install Lotus Notes, the database icons have a three-dimensional appearance and the Workspace looks marbled or textured. You can change this default appearance and show the Workspace background as plain gray, with the database icons appearing as simple squares. Try using Notes with the textured setting for a while and then switch to the plain setting to decide which you like best.

Setting Options for Trash

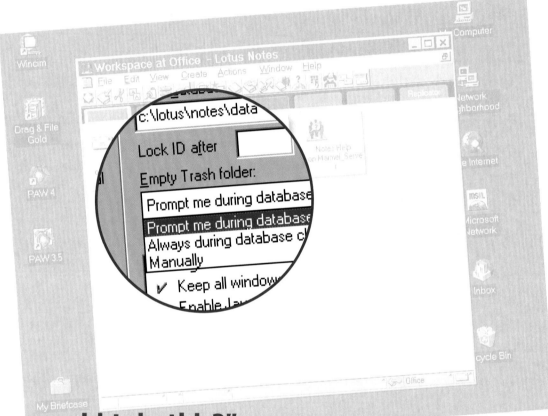

"Why would I do this?"

When you mark a document for deletion, Notes does not immediately delete the document. By default, Notes waits until you exit the database and prompts you to delete marked documents as you exit. You can change this default so that Notes prompts you in any of the following ways:

- If you choose Manually, you will need to place documents you want to delete in the Trash folder or mark them for deletion.

Then, press **F9** to refresh the screen and actually delete the documents.

- If you choose Prompt me during database close, Notes displays a reminder message asking if you want to delete marked documents. Choose **Yes** or **No**, as appropriate.

- If you choose Always during database close, Notes deletes all documents you marked when you close the database without prompting you.

206

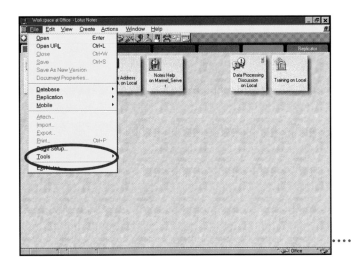

1 Open the **File** menu and choose **Tools**.

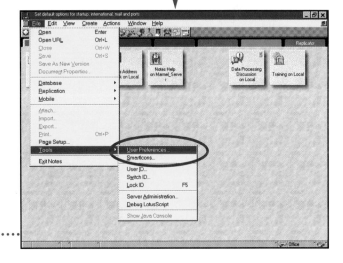

2 From the **Tools** menu, choose **User Preferences**.

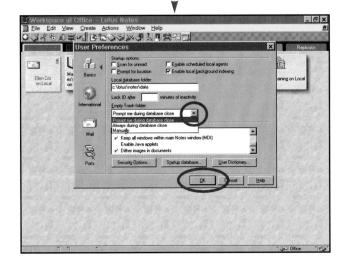

3 In the User Preferences dialog box, open the **Empty Trash folder** list box to select an option. Choose **OK** to save your selection. ∎

TASK 73

Keeping Copies of Mail You Send

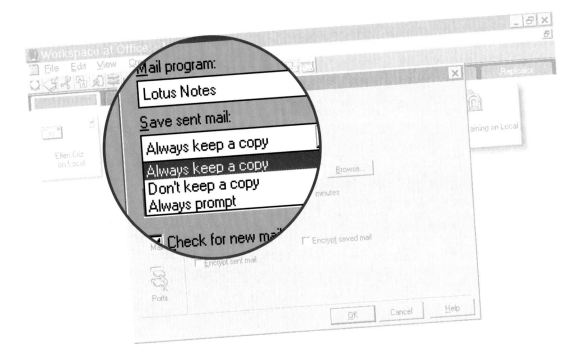

"Why would I do this?"

You can tell Notes to keep a copy of any e-mail you send. By default, Notes keeps a copy of all the mail you send. You can choose not to keep a copy or to be prompted about keeping a copy.

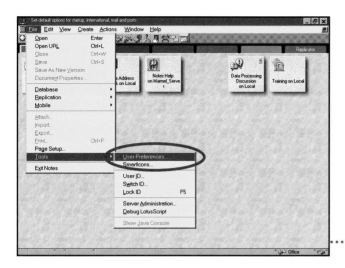

1 Open the **File** menu and choose **Tools**. From the Tools menu, choose **User Preferences**.

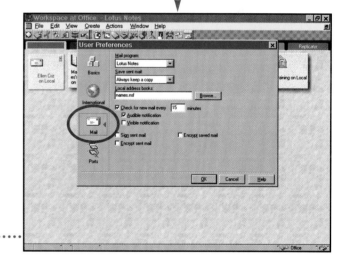

2 In the User Preferences dialog box, click the **Mail** icon at the left side of the box to see mail options.

3 Open the **Save sent mail** list box to see your choices. After you make a selection, choose **OK** to save it. ∎

209

TASK

74

Modifying Workspace Tabs

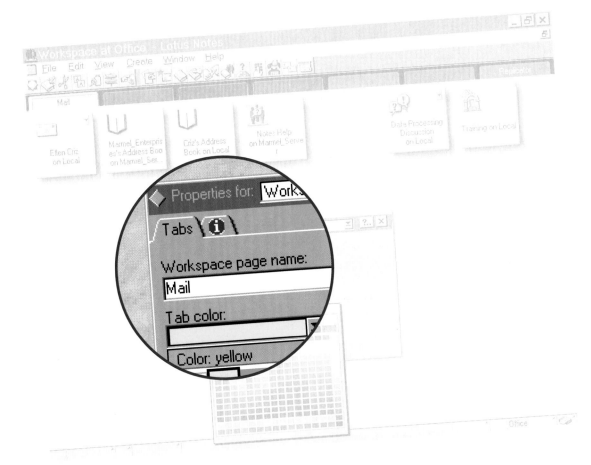

"Why would I do this?"

Your Workspace contains six unlabeled tabs. Each of the tabs is a different color. You can label each tab and change the color of the tabs. Then, as you'll learn in the next task, you can move databases between the tabs. Using these two techniques, you'll be able to organize your Notes Workspace to suit your work style.

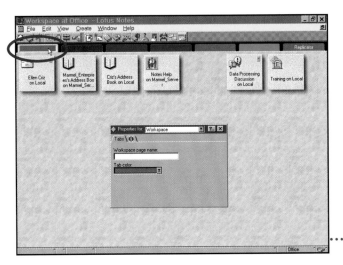

1 Double-click the Workspace tab you want to modify. The Workspace Properties InfoBox appears.

2 To label the tab, type a name for the Workspace tab in the Workspace page name text box. As you move out of the field, Notes updates the tab.

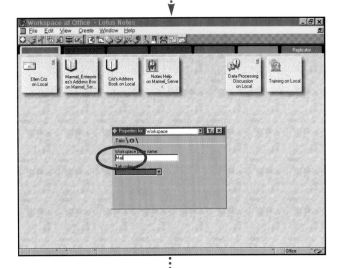

Puzzled?

To label and change the color of other tabs, just click the tab while the Workspace Properties InfoBox is open. Notes will show information for the currently displayed tab.

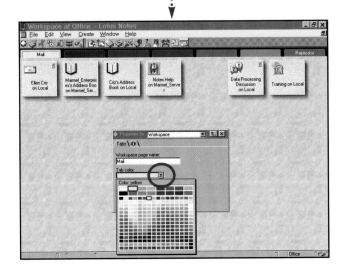

3 To change the tab color, open the Tab color list box and select a color. Notes updates the tab before you close the InfoBox. Choose the **Close** (**X**) button to close the Properties InfoBox. ■

TASK

75

Moving Databases Between Workspace Pages

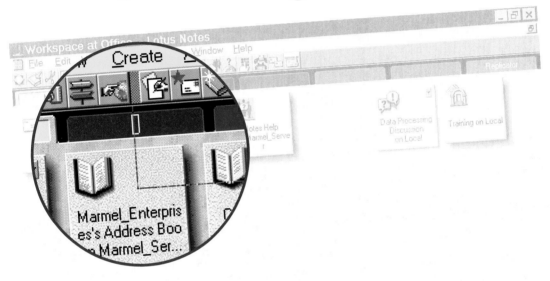

"Why would I do this?"

As you create more and more databases, you'll want to organize them on the Workspace tabs. Since you've already learned how to name your Workspace tabs, in this task, you'll learn how to move databases between Workspace tabs so that you can "group" like databases together.

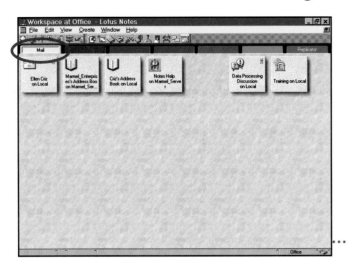

1 Display the Workspace tab containing the database you'd like to move.

2 Highlight the database you want to move, drag it up to the Workspace tab on which you want to place it, and drop it. As you drag, the mouse pointer will change to a hand and you'll see the outline of the database icon.

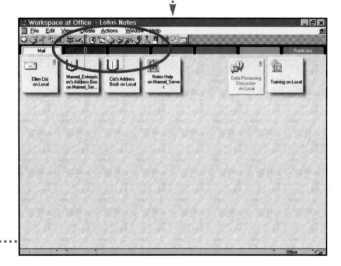

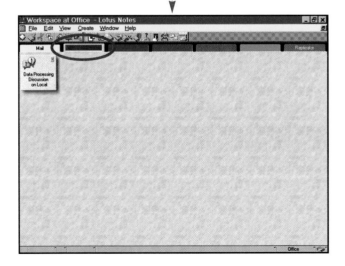

Puzzled?

You can identify the tab Notes has selected because you'll see a small white square in the center of the selected tab as you drag the database onto a tab.

3 Click the tab onto which you moved the database to see the database on that tab. ∎

Changing Your Personal Password

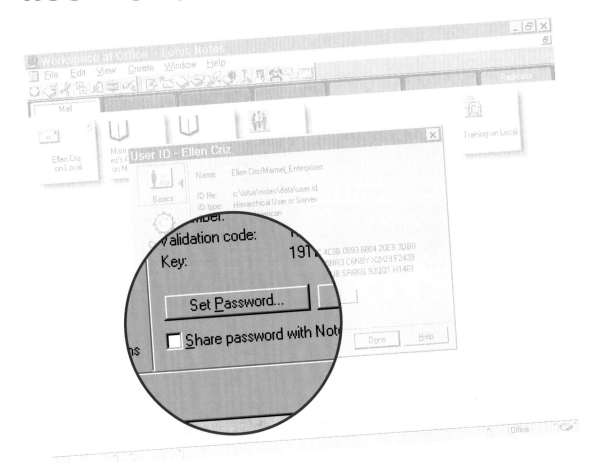

"Why would I do this?"

Although you don't need a Notes password to access information located on your local machine, you do need one to access information on your server. Your system administrator gives you your first password, but you can change it and you should. Your password can be any set of characters you want as long as it begins with a letter.

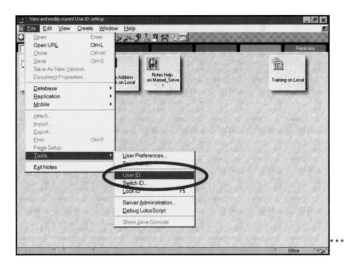

1 Open the **File** menu and choose **Tools**. From the Tools submenu, choose **User ID**.

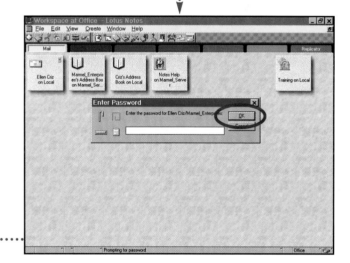

2 Notes prompts you for your current password. After you supply your password, choose **OK**.

3 Notes displays the User ID dialog box, where you can set your password. Click the **Set Password** command button.

4 Notes displays the Enter Password dialog box. This is the same dialog box Notes prompted you for in Step 2 and appears at the top of the figure next to this step. Type your current password and choose **OK**. Notes displays the Set Password dialog box.

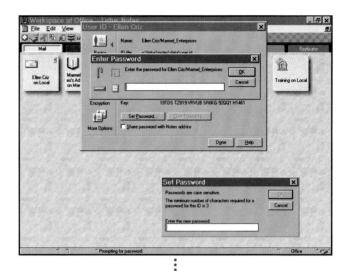

Puzzled?

Your administrator controls the required length of your password. You may see a different number, such as 8, for the minimum number of required characters.

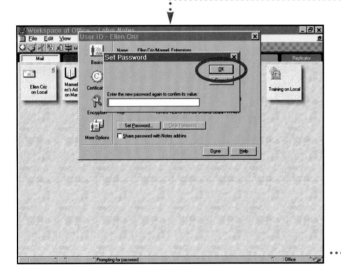

5 Type your new password and choose **OK**. Notes displays the Set Password dialog box again and asks you to confirm the password by typing it again. Type your new password again and click **OK**.

6 Notes redisplays the User ID dialog box, from which you can choose **Done**. ■

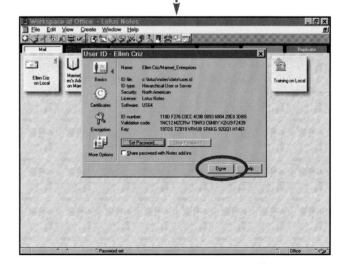

TASK

77

Changing Your Workspace Background

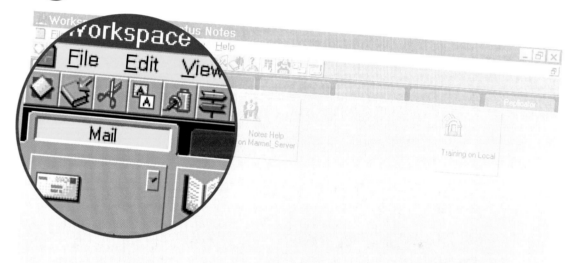

"Why would I do this?"

Throughout this book, the Workspace background appears as textured, and database icons have a three-dimensional appearance. And, by default, Lotus ships Notes showing the Workspace background as textured and database icons as three-dimensional. You can,

however, choose to display the Workspace background as plain gray, with the database icons appearing as simple squares. You can switch between these two settings to decide which you like best.

Task 77: Changing Your Workspace Background

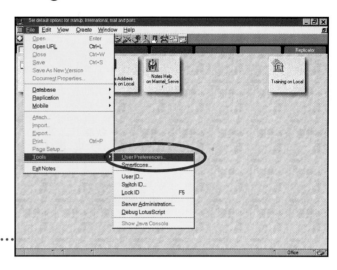

1 Open the **File** menu and choose the **Tools** command. From the submenu, choose **User Preferences**.

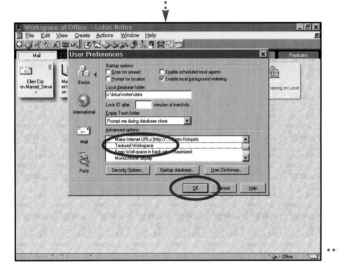

2 In the User Preferences dialog box that appears, search the Advanced options list box until you find Textured Workspace.

3 If you click the choice to remove the check next to the option and choose **OK**, the Notes Workspace will appear plain and database icons will appear as simple squares like the ones in this figure. ∎

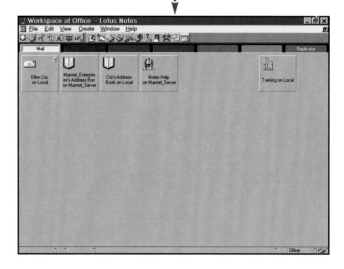

PART VIII

Reference

- Installing Notes on a Workstation
- Glossary

Installing Notes on a Workstation

Following are the steps you can use to install Lotus Notes to a local area network (LAN) workstation, connected to the server with cables, or as a dial-up workstation, connected to the server by phone lines.

The Notes server must be up and running before you install Notes to the LAN workstation. Additionally, you should temporarily disable any screen savers and virus-detection software; make sure no programs are running on the workstation. As you install the software, you may need additional information such as your password; contact your system administrator.

To install notes on a Windows 95 workstation, follow these steps:

1. From the Windows 95 desktop, choose the **Start** button and the **Run** command.

2. Insert the Lotus CD or disk 1 in the drive and enter the drive:\directory\install command (for example, d:\win32\install) and press **Enter**. If you're using floppy disks to install, insert new disks in the floppy drive as prompted.

3. When prompted, enter your name and company name, and choose **Next**.

4. Choose **Yes** to confirm the names or **No** to re-enter them.

5. When prompted, choose the **Standard Install** option and choose **Next**.

6. Continue installation, answering the on-screen prompts as necessary.

Glossary

ACL (Access Control List) The list of users allowed to use a database. The ACL lists who is allowed to access the database and what kind of access they have. Access can range from No Access to Manager.

Action bar The bar of buttons that contains various actions you can take, such as Create a New Document. Typically, you'll see an Action bar above the View pane, but you might also see an Action bar in a document.

Address Book A database that contains the names and e-mail addresses of Notes users. It can also include physical addresses and phone numbers. The Address Book on the Server contains the names and e-mail addresses of all Notes users on the network. Notes uses the Address Book to route mail.

attachment A file included in a Notes document. To send a file to another Notes user, you can send the file as an attachment in an e-mail message.

BCC (Blind Carbon Copy) Sends a copy of an e-mail message to a recipient(s) whose name(s) and address(es) appear in the BCC field without any of the other recipients being aware of it.

CC (Carbon Copy) Sends a copy of an e-mail message to the recipient(s) whose name(s) and address(es) appear in the CC field.

client A computer or workstation that connects to a server. Usually, your computer is a client that connects to a server located somewhere else.

database A Notes file, represented by a database icon. Notes databases are like compartments and store documents. Typically, databases are located on servers and accessed by clients from all over the network. You can read a description of a particular database using the About button in the Open Database dialog box.

database design Determines how the users read, input, and modify information in a database. A database design consists of design elements such as fields, forms, views, and agents (formerly called "macros").

database icon Square icon that represents a Notes database. Database icons contain pictures and descriptive titles. Optionally, the number of unread messages can be displayed on the icon.

DocLink A small icon that appears in a database document. When you double-click the DocLink icon, Notes switches to the document referenced by the DocLink.

document A completed form in a Notes database.

field A place in a document containing information. Some fields allow you to type into them, and others have formulas that perform calculations.

form The foundation of a document. The form determines how fields are displayed and how information can be entered into them.

full text index A listing of all words in the database you can use to search documents in a database.

full text search A query against the full text index to locate documents matching specified words, phrases, numbers, or dates.

groupware An application that helps people work collaboratively with electronic information. Lotus222 Notes is an example of groupware.

LAN (Local Area Network) Servers and clients connected by cables or telephone wires for the purpose of sharing data. The servers typically stay logged on to the LAN, so that the information in their databases can be accessed at any time. Clients typically log on and off of the LAN as necessary.

modem A device that attaches to a computer to allow for remote communication via phone lines.

Navigation pane The area on the left side of the screen when you open a database. The Navigation pane may contain icons or folders. use the Navigation pane to switch folders and display database contents in different ways.

password An encrypted text string that permits use of a user ID to authorized persons and, conversely, denies use of a user ID to unauthorized persons. Typically, Notes users each have a single User ID, which they do not share.

pop-up Area on a document that you can click for additional information. The document's author can place pop-ups almost anywhere on the document. Usually, you see pop-ups as a green rectangle surrounding text.

Preview pane A pane that can appear at the bottom of the screen. The Preview pane displays the contents of the document currently highlighted in the View pane.

record A record is the same thing as a document. See *document*.

remote workstation A computer that connects to the network via modem.

server A computer that stores data for use by clients. In Notes, the server also authenticates your user ID when you attempt to access the server; you must have a valid user ID in order to access any server. Notes databases are typically located on servers.

SmartIcons A row of small square icons (default location is at the top of the screen) that you can click to perform Notes menu commands.

template A database without records that you can use as a model when creating a new database. Templates contain a complete set of design elements. Notes ships with many templates. You see a list of available templates on your own machine in the New Database dialog box. If you switch to the server, you'll see a list of templates available on the server in the New Database dialog box.

User ID An encrypted, unique password that allows the person who knows the password access to Notes servers and databases.

view A display of documents in a database. Views contain documents that are sorted, totaled, or grouped together in almost any logical manner.

View pane The right side of the screen when you open a database. The View pane typically lists documents, and the order of the documents depends on which folder you select in the Navigation pane.

Workspace The window displayed when Notes is first activated. The Workspace has seven tabbed pages, including the Replicator tab. You can view the different contents of a Workspace tab by clicking the tab.

Index

C

Index

D

data, importing into documents, 149
Database command (File menu), 111, 165
databases, 110, 222
    adding
        documents, 122
        to workspace, 112-113
    categories, 152-153
    copying, 114-115
    deleting documents, 206
    discussion groups, 162
    DocLinks, 143-144
    forwarding messages, 50-51
    icons, 20
    local replicas, 183, 194-196
    locating on servers, 111
    Mail, 184, 200
    moving between Workspace pages, 212-213
    opening with mouse, 12
    redisplaying, 119
    removing from workspace, 159-160
    replication, 183, 194-196
    searches, 116-118
        complex conditions, 119
        full text indexes, 117
        Search Bar, 15
    updating remote changes, 201-203
date of creation views of documents, 156
Delegate To dialog box, 98
Delegation Profile, 76, 184
Delete button, 47
deleting
    databases from workspace, 159-160
    document preference settings, 206
    mail, 46
delivery options for messages, 57-59
desktop, wallpaper display, 9
detaching documents from mail, 37-38
dial-up connections, 182, 198

dialog boxes
    Call Server, 198
    Create Attachment, 62
    Delegate To, 98
    File Print, 42
    Free Time, 92
    Mail Address, 57
    Move to Folder, 44-45
    Name, 65
    Open Database, 111
    Quick Search, 22
    Save Attachment, 38
    Search Builder, 117
    Select Keywords, 153
    Time and Phone Information for Travel, 191
Dictionary, adding words, 141
digital signature, message options, 59
discussion groups, 162
    anonymous response documents, 175-176
    categorizing documents, 168
    interest profiles, 163, 178-179
    joining, 164-165
    main documents, 163, 168-169
    New Main Topic button, 168
    organization options, 166
    posting messages, 167
    response documents, 163, 170
    response to response documents, 163, 172
    threads, 178
    view options, 164
Discussion template, 163
Display Invitee responsees button, 95
displaying
    Action bar, 14
    context sensitive help, 18
    help topics, 21
    Inbox, 30
    quick menus, 12
    Search Bar, 16
    SmartIcon bar, 14
DocLinks, 143-144, 222
    documents
        testing, 145
Document Preview command (View menu), 121

documents, 222
    About This Database, 111
    adding to databases, 122
    anonymous response documents in discussion groups, 175-176
    attaching messages, 60, 62
    deleting preference settings, 206
    detaching mail, 37
    discussion groups, categorizing, 168
    DocLinks, 143-144
    editing, 125
    formatting, 129
    hotspots, 146
    importing data, 149
    lists, 130
    Location, remote Notes settings, 188
    main documents in discussion groups, 163, 168-170
    marking unread as read, 118
    organizing by categories, 153
    previewing, 120
    printing from views, 157
    redisplaying, 119
    response documents, 163, 170
    response to response documents, 163, 172
    saving, 122
    Server Connection, 192-193
    tables, 135
    tabs, 132
    text
        copying, 124-125
        cutting, 125
        finding, 137
        formatting, 128
        moving, 124
        pasting, 125
        replacing, 137
        Spell Checker, 140
    Travel Location, 191
    Undo feature, 126
    viewing options, 155

Index

documents
    copying, 125
    formatting, 128
    importing, 149
    pasting, 125
    Spell Checker, 140
    tabs, 132
    underlining, 129
    undoing changes, 127
  finding and replacing, 137
  moving, 124
  pasting, 125
  searching for in databases, 118
Text Bold SmartIcon, 129
text boxes, password appearance, 10-11
Text menu commands, 129
Text Properties InfoBox, tab stops, 133
textured Workspace background, 218
threads in discussion groups, 178
Time and Phone Information for Travel dialog box, 191
titles for documents, 123
To Do List
  creating, 99
  dates/times, 100
  Mark Completed button, 106
  New Task button, 100
  Please Reassign button, 102
  Priority option button, 100
  Remove from To Do View, 106
  tasks, reassigning, 102
  text description, 100
  views, 101, 105-106
Trash, document deletion options, 207
Travel Location document, 191
travel uses for Lotus Notes, 182
Two Days button (Calendar), 79
Two Weeks button (Calendar), 79

U

undeleting mail, 46
underlining text in documents, 129
Undo feature, 126-127
unread documents, marking as read, 118
updating remote database changes, 201-203
User IDs, 215-216, 223

V

View menu commands
  Document Preview, 121
  Search Bar, 16, 118
View pane, 223
  Inbox, 30
  Notes Help, 19
View Show/Hide Show Search Bar SmartIcon, 15
viewing
  Calendar
    appointment times, 79
    Calendar Profile access section, 76
    formats, 77-79
  documents, 155
  mail, 30-31
  To Do List, 101
views, 223
  All Documents, 156
  discussion group options, 164
  DocLinks, 145
  printing documents from, 157

W-Z

wallpapers, Windows 95 display options, 9
windows, maximizing or minimizing, 23
Windows 95
  installing Lotus Notes, 220
  wallpapers, 9
words, adding to dictionary, 141
Workspace, 223
  adding databases, 112-113
  background options, 217
  color options for tabs, 211
  customizing, 204
  label options for tabs, 210-211
  moving databases between pages and tabs, 212-213
  removing databases from workspace, 159-160
  Workspace pages, 11
workstations
  copying databases, 114-115
  installing Lotus Notes, 220

Check out Que® Books on the World Wide Web
http://www.mcp.com/que

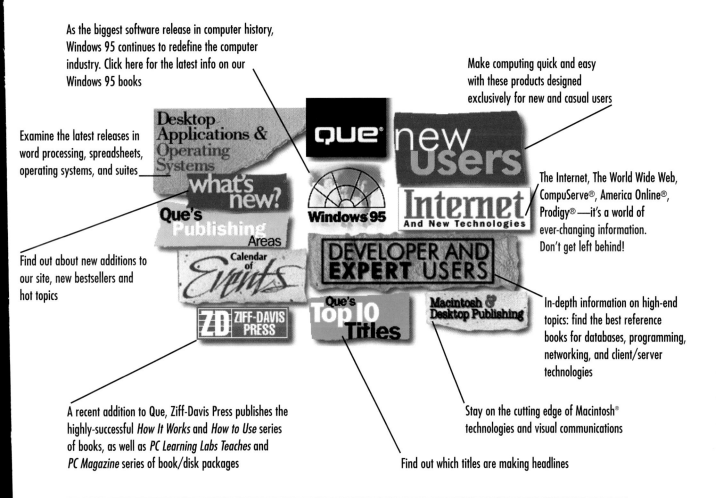

As the biggest software release in computer history, Windows 95 continues to redefine the computer industry. Click here for the latest info on our Windows 95 books

Make computing quick and easy with these products designed exclusively for new and casual users

Examine the latest releases in word processing, spreadsheets, operating systems, and suites

The Internet, The World Wide Web, CompuServe®, America Online®, Prodigy®—it's a world of ever-changing information. Don't get left behind!

Find out about new additions to our site, new bestsellers and hot topics

In-depth information on high-end topics: find the best reference books for databases, programming, networking, and client/server technologies

A recent addition to Que, Ziff-Davis Press publishes the highly-successful *How It Works* and *How to Use* series of books, as well as *PC Learning Labs Teaches* and *PC Magazine* series of book/disk packages

Stay on the cutting edge of Macintosh® technologies and visual communications

Find out which titles are making headlines

With 6 separate publishing groups, Que develops products for many specific market segments and areas of computer technology. Explore our Web Site and you'll find information on best-selling titles, newly published titles, upcoming products, authors, and much more.

- Stay informed on the latest industry trends and products available
- Visit our online bookstore for the latest information and editions
- Download software from Que's library of the best shareware and freeware

Copyright © 1996, Macmillan Computer Publishing-USA, A Viacom Company

MACMILLAN COMPUTER PUBLISHING USA

A VIACOM COMPANY

Technical Support:

If you need assistance with the information in this book or with a CD/Disk accompanying the book, please access the Knowledge Base on our Web site at **http://www.superlibrary.com/general/support**. Our most Frequently Asked Questions are answered there. If you do not find the answer to your questions on our Web site, you may contact Macmillan Technical Support **(317) 581-3833** or e-mail us at **support@mcp.com**.